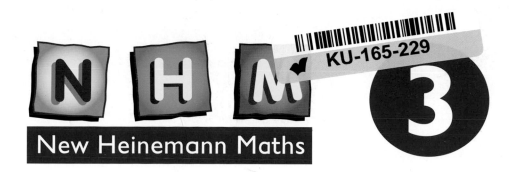

Textbook

Heinemann Educational Publishers
Halley Court, Jordan Hill, Oxford, OX2 8EJ
a division of Reed Educational and Professional Publishing Ltd

Heinemann is a registered trademark of Reed Educational and Professional Publishing Ltd

Writing team

John T Blair

Percy W Farren

Myra A Pearson

Dorothy S Simpson

John W Thayers

David K Thomson

First published 2000

10 09 08 07
14 13 12 11

ISBN 978 0 435171 98 8

Produced by Gecko Ltd.
Illustrated by Phil Garner, Shelagh McNicholas, Lorna Kent and Gecko Ltd.
Printed and bound in China through Phoenix Offset

Contents

1

(a) 9 + 4   (b) 5 + 7   (c) 8 + 8   (d) 9 + 2

(e) 8 + 5   (f) 3 + 8   (g) 9 + 0   (h) 10 + 7

2 How many altogether?

(a) 8   3

(b) 5   9

(c) 10   6

3 Add two ◇ each time.

(a) Make 14.

7   6
8   9

(b) Make 17.

8   10
9   5

(c) Make 15.

9   5
8   6

4

(a) $9 + \blacksquare = 16$ (b) $6 + \blacksquare = 12$ (c) $\blacksquare + \triangle = 12$

(d) $\blacksquare + 9 = 13$ (e) $\blacksquare + 8 = 18$ (f) $\blacksquare + \triangle = 11$

1

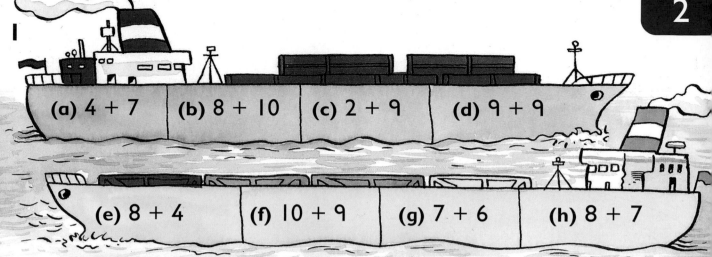

(a) 4 + 7 (b) 8 + 10 (c) 2 + 9 (d) 9 + 9

(e) 8 + 4 (f) 10 + 9 (g) 7 + 6 (h) 8 + 7

2

5 crabs on the rock.
6 crabs in the pool.
How many altogether?

3 How many fish?

(a) 3 9

(b) 5 8

(c) 10 5

4

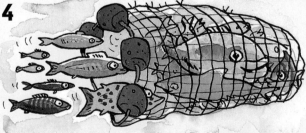

7 fish in the net.
7 more swim in.
How many now?

5 Use two ▱ each time.
What totals can be made?

9 6 7 8

9 + 6 =
9 + 7

1 Write the number **1 more than**

(a) 11   (b) 18   (c) 14   (d) 19   (e) 16

2 Write the number **2 more than**

   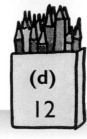 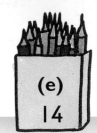

(a) 13   (b) 17   (c) 15   (d) 12   (e) 14

3 Add the numbers on

(a) the **red** bibs   (b) the **blue** bibs

(c) the **green** bibs   (d) the **yellow** bibs.

4 (a) $12 + 4$ (b) $6 + 13$ (c) $14 + 5$

  (d) $7 + 11$ (e) $2 + 16$ (f) $11 + 3$

5 (a) $15 + \blacksquare = 19$ (b) $1 + \blacksquare = 18$ (c) $\blacksquare + 2 = 13$

1 Add 10.

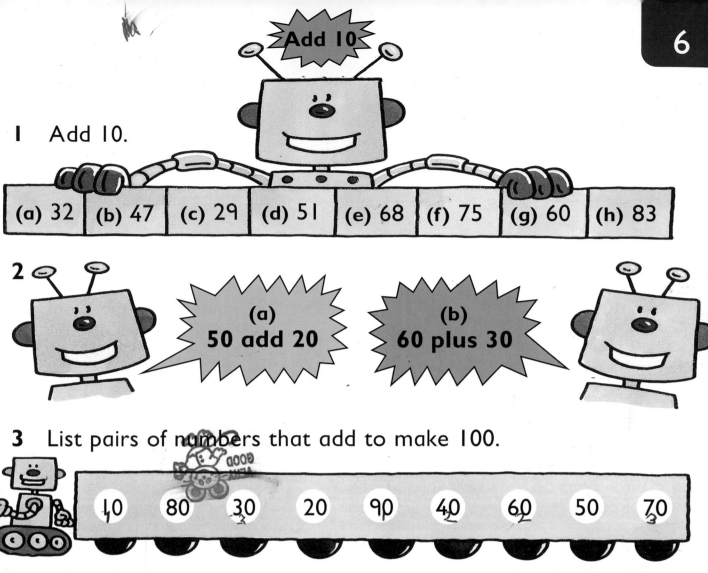

(a) 32 | (b) 47 | (c) 29 | (d) 51 | (e) 68 | (f) 75 | (g) 60 | (h) 83

2

(a)
50 add 20

(b)
60 plus 30

3 List pairs of numbers that add to make 100.

10   80   30   20   90   40   60   50   70

4

(a) 35 + 40   (b) 50 + 29   (c) 63 + 30

(d) 70 + 18   (e) 20 + 75   (f) 31 + 60

5

(a) 24 + ■ = 64   (b) 46 + ■ = 76

(c) 20 + ■ = 90   (d) ■ + 15 = 45

(e) ■ + 70 = 91   (f) ■ + 19 = 79

1 Add 11.

(a) 28
(b) 45
(c) 57
(d) 73

2 Add 9.

(a) 28
(b) 55
(c) 62
(d) 86

3 Add 21.

(a) 48 | (b) 54 | (c) 66 | (d) 72

4 Add 19.

(a) 22 | (b) 35 | (c) 59 | (d) 73

5 (a) 25 + 29 | 25 + 30 = 55 | (b) 25 + 31

6 (a) 33 + 29 | (b) 33 + 31

7
(a) 42 + 49 | (b) 37 + 31 | (c) 26 + 59 | (d) 48 + 51
(e) 44 + 41 | (f) 17 + 39 | (g) 28 + 69 | (h) 29 + 61

1

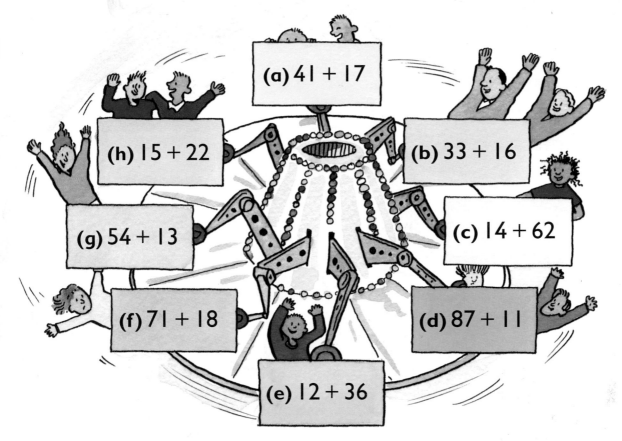

(a) 41 + 17

(h) 15 + 22

(b) 33 + 16

(g) 54 + 13

(c) 14 + 62

(f) 71 + 18

(d) 87 + 11

(e) 12 + 36

2 Write each child's total.

Bob 32 16

Fifi 15 24

May 46 14

3 Find the missing numbers.

(a) 26 + ▨ = 37

(b) 42 + ▨ = 59

(c) ▨ + 18 = 49

(d) ▨ + 13 = 66

1

(a) 22 + 36

(b) 41 + 48

(c) 33 + 55

(d) 24 + 34

(e) 61 + 25

2

(a) 25 + 53

(b) 71 + 27

(c) 56 + 23

(d) 43 + 52

(e) 23 + 37

Pete

Paint needed

36 litres   27 litres

23 litres   32 litres

3 How many litres altogether are there when Pete mixes

(a) the red and blue paint   (b) the yellow and green paint

(c) the yellow and red paint   (d) the green and blue paint?

4

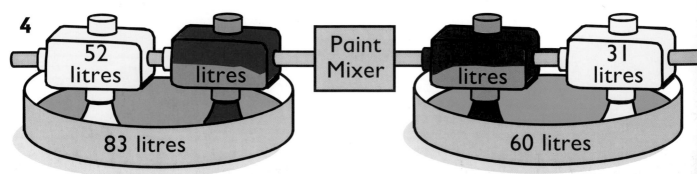

52 litres   litres   Paint Mixer   litres   31 litres

83 litres   60 litres

(a) How many litres of red paint?

(b) How many litres of blue paint?

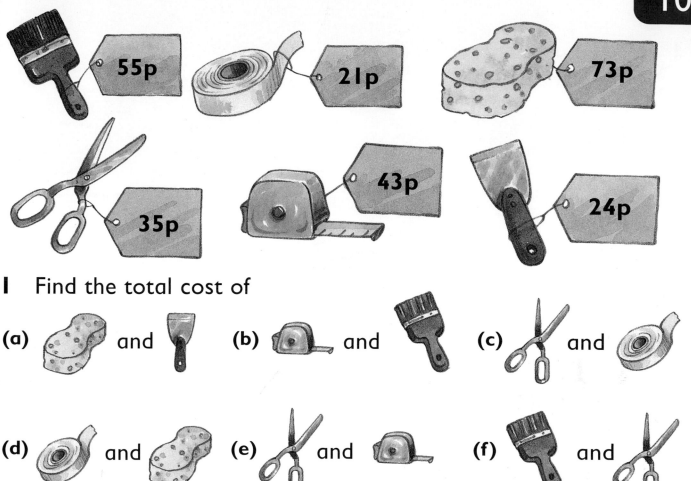

Price tags:
- paint brush 55p
- tape 21p
- sponge 73p
- scissors 35p
- tape measure 43p
- scraper 24p

1 Find the total cost of

(a) sponge and scraper

(b) tape measure and paint brush

(c) scissors and tape

(d) tape and sponge

(e) scissors and tape measure

(f) paint brush and scissors

2 Draw (a) **two** things you can buy for 45p
(b) **three** things you can buy for 80p.

3 Make 100.

(a) 55 + ■

(b) ■ + 5

(c) 75 + ■

(d) 35 + ■

100

(e) ■ + 45

(f) ■ + 85

1 How much altogether?

(a)

(b)

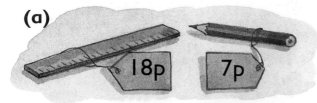

2

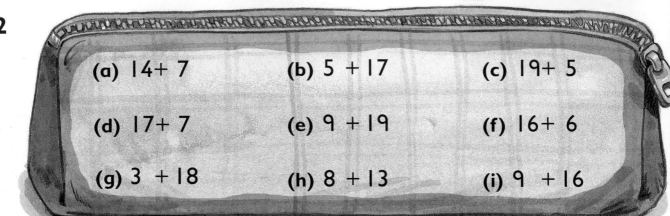

(a) 14+ 7   (b) 5 +17   (c) 19+ 5

(d) 17+ 7   (e) 9 +19   (f) 16+ 6

(g) 3 +18   (h) 8 +13   (i) 9 +16

3 Find each total.

(a)   (b)   (c)

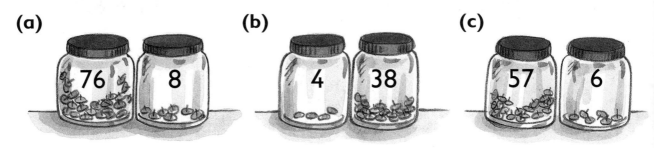

4 (a) Add 85 and 7.   (b) 8 plus 44   (c) 26 add 5

(d) Find the sum of 57 and 4.   (e) Add 8 to 66.

5 What must be added

(a) to 78 to make 81   (b) to 7 to make 35

(c) to 88 to make 96   (d) to 3 to make 100?

65 passengers   17 passengers

1   How many passengers altogether?

2   Find the total.

(a) 14   38   (b) 16   46

3   **(a)** 73 + 18   **(b)** 15 + 76   **(c)** 14 + 67

    (d) 28 + 17   **(e)** 48 + 18   **(f)** 59 + 13

      (g)   36 + ■ = 52   **(h)**   ■ + 27 = 45

4   Choose one **adult** ticket and one **child** ticket
    each time. Find the total cost.

adult	adult	child	child
45p	**68p**	**15p**	**17p**

adult	adult	adult	adult
77p	**56p**	**18p**	**16p**

1 Add the numbers on
(a) the **blue** helmets
(b) the **red** helmets.

2 Find the sum of the numbers on cars of the **same colour.**

26

27

52

44

73

48

29

68

3 (a) 63 + 28   (b) 35 + 26   (c) 48 + 25

(d) 37 + 54   (e) 46 + 36   (f) 38 + 38

(g) 67 + ■ = 91   (h) 25 + ■ = 72

1 Find the total cost of

(a)

(b)

(c)

(d)

(e)

(f)

2 (a) $15 + 6 + 15 + 1$ (b) $5 + 11 + 12 + 4$

(c) $12 + 7 + 8 + 9$ (d) $6 + 7 + 4 + 2 + 7$

3 Copy and complete.

(a) $17 + \blacksquare + 3 = 32$ (b) $7 + \blacksquare + 11 = 22$

(c) $\blacksquare + 13 + 13 = 34$ (d) $19 + 5 + \blacksquare + 10 = 39$

(e) $19 + \blacksquare + \triangle = 30$ (f) $\blacksquare + \triangle + \diamondsuit = 40$

4 Write five **different** numbers that add up to 35.

1 Find different ways to make 20.

(a) Use **two** numbers each time.

9	5	10
4	7	15
13	16	11

(b) Use **three** numbers each time.

15	4	11
3	10	7
2	13	1

(c) Use **four** numbers each time.

6	9	3
7	8	1
2	5	4

2 Write the missing numbers.

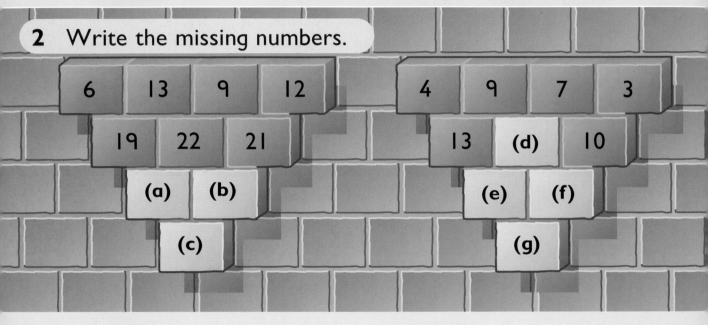

6	13	9	12

19	22	21

(a) (b)

(c)

4	9	7	3

13	(d)	10

(e) (f)

(g)

3 Find each total.

(a)  → Double it. → Add 26. → Add 1 less than 40.

(b) → Add 10. → Add the sum of 2 and 17. → Add the total of 7 and 5.

(c) → Double it. → Add 29. → Add double 8.

1 Find the missing numbers.

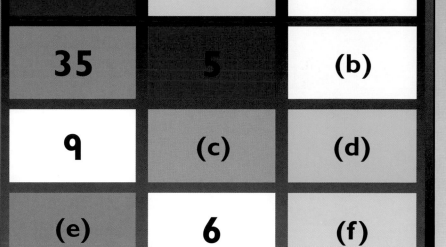

(a)	63	36
35	5	(b)
9	(c)	(d)
(e)	6	(f)
42	25	(g)

☐ + ☐ = 19   ☐ + ☐ = 76

☐ + ☐ = 74   ☐ + ☐ = 65

☐ + ☐ = 100   ☐ + ☐ = 80

☐ + ☐ + ☐ = 30

2 Find the total of

(a) the **blue** boxes and the **white** boxes

(b) the **red** boxes and the **yellow** boxes.

1

(a)	11 – 6	**(e)**	18 – 9	**(i)**	12 – 4
(b)	17 – 8	**(f)**	13 – 8	**(j)**	16 – 7
(c)	14 – 7	**(g)**	11 – 3	**(k)**	15 – 9
(d)	13 – 6	**(h)**	14 – 5	**(l)**	12 – 7

2

(a) 17 🐟
9 are stolen.
How many are left?

(b) 13 🐟
7 are eaten.
How many are left?

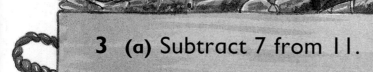

3 **(a)** Subtract 7 from 11.   **(b)** Take 9 from 16.

     (c) 15 minus 8   **(d)** 12 subtract 8

4 **(a)** $14 - \blacksquare = 5$ **(b)** $12 - \blacksquare = 6$ **(c)** $11 - \blacksquare = 7$

    (d) $\blacksquare - 8 = 8$ **(e)** $\blacksquare - 5 = 8$ **(f)** $\blacksquare - 4 = 9$

1

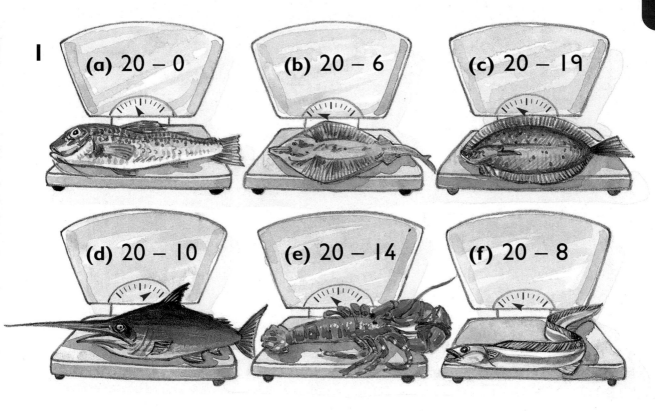

(a) 20 – 0   (b) 20 – 6   (c) 20 – 19

(d) 20 – 10   (e) 20 – 14   (f) 20 – 8

2 (a) 20 – 2   (b) 20 – 7   (c) 20 – 1

    (d) 20 – 5   (e) 20 – 11   (f) 20 – 13

3

Ann: I have 3 left.

Tom: I have 11 left.

20 sole

20 cod

How many fish have been sold by (a) Ann (b) Tom?

4 (a) 12 less than 20   (b) 16 fewer than 20

    (c) Subtract 15 from 20.   (d) 3 less than 20

    (e) Take 20 from 20.   (f) 20 minus 4

Harbour Museum

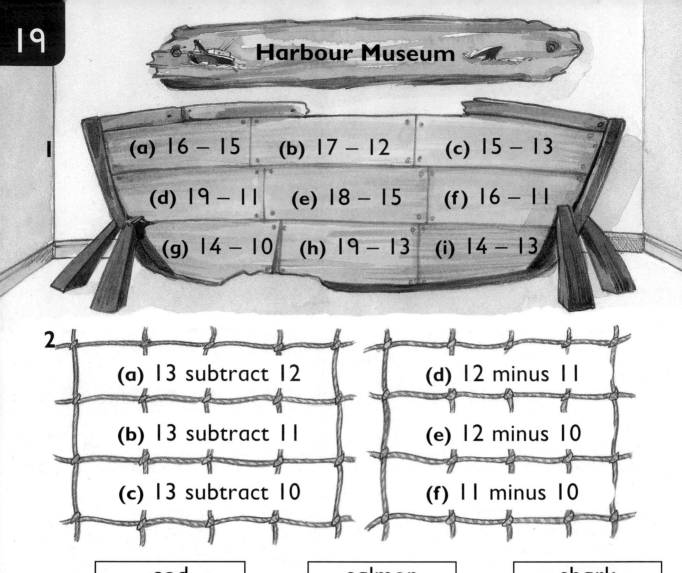

1
(a) 16 – 15　　(b) 17 – 12　　(c) 15 – 13

(d) 19 – 11　　(e) 18 – 15　　(f) 16 – 11

(g) 14 – 10　　(h) 19 – 13　　(i) 14 – 13

2
(a) 13 subtract 12　　　　(d) 12 minus 11

(b) 13 subtract 11　　　　(e) 12 minus 10

(c) 13 subtract 10　　　　(f) 11 minus 10

3

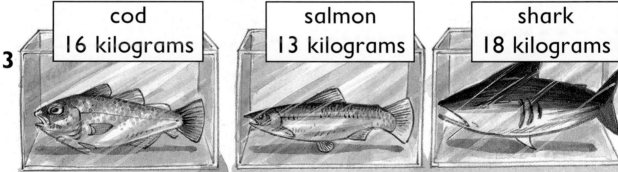

cod
16 kilograms

salmon
13 kilograms

shark
18 kilograms

Find the difference in weight between
(a) the shark and the cod
(b) the shark and the salmon
(c) the salmon and the cod.

4　(a) 19 – ■ = 5　　　(b) 17 – ■ = 4　　　(c) 15 – ■ = 3

Museum shop

18p 12p 16p 17p 19p 14p

1 Find the difference in price between

(a) 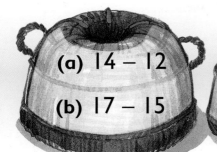 and **(b)** and **(c)** and

(d) and **(e)** and **(f)** and

2

(a) 14 − 12   (c) 15 − 11   (e) 16 − 12
(b) 17 − 15   (d) 18 − 14   (f) 15 − 14

3 (a) 19 minus 15 (b) 17 subtract 16
(c) Take 10 from 16. (d) Subtract 11 from 14.
(e) 18 take away 12 (f) 19 minus 17

4

(a) 18 − ■ = 7 (b) 17 − ■ = 6
(c) ■ − 14 = 2 (d) ■ − 10 = 9

1 Copy and complete.

 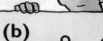 

(a)
7 – 2 = ▪
17 – 2 = ▪
27 – 2 = ▪
57 – 2 = ▪

(b)
9 – 6 = ▪
19 – 6 = ▪
29 – 6 = ▪
89 – 6 = ▪

(c)
8 – 5 = ▪
18 – 5 = ▪
28 – 5 = ▪
78 – 5 = ▪

2 Subtract 7.

(a)  68 **(b)**  39 **(c)**  97 **(d)** 29

3 Subtract 3.

(a) 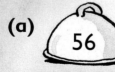 56 **(b)**  77 **(c)** 35 **(d)**  48

4 (a) 69 grapes.
5 are eaten.
How many are left?

(b) 36 dates.
4 are eaten.
How many are left?

5 (a) Take 2 from 45.   **(b)** 58 subtract 4

(c) Subtract 6 from 97.   **(d)** 69 minus 8

6 (a) 47 – ▪ = 43   **(b)** 68 – ▪ = 65   **(c)** ▪ – 6 = 82

1 Subtract 10 from

(a) 47

(b) 58

(c) 64

2 50 less than

(a) 85

(b) 59

(c) 91

3 Take 30 from

(a) 32

(b) 86

(c) 73

4 (a) $72 - 60 = \blacksquare$

(b) $84 - 40 = \blacksquare$

(c) $83 - 70 = \blacksquare$

(d) $57 - 30 = \blacksquare$

5 (a) $69 - 40 = \blacksquare$

(b) $43 - 20 = \blacksquare$

(c) $99 - 80 = \blacksquare$

(d) $60 - 30 = \blacksquare$

6 (a) $56 - \blacksquare = 36$

(b) $71 - \blacksquare = 31$

(c) $\blacksquare - 30 = 65$

(d) $\blacksquare - 60 = 28$

1 Subtract 11 from
(a) 38
(b) 64
(c) 85

2 Subtract 21 from
(a) 49
(b) 73
(c) 57

3 Subtract 9 from
(a) 26
(b) 65
(c) 94

4 Subtract 19 from
(a) 78
(b) 33
(c) 52

5 (a) 77 – 39   (b) 66 – 51

(c) 87 – 61   (d) 91 – 79

(e) 62 – 41   (f) 60 – 39

6 (a) 95 take away 31   (b) 84 subtract 49

(c) Take 29 from 46.   (d) Subtract 31 from 80.

7 92 soldiers.
59 are riding on horses.
How many are on foot?

1 There were **48** questions in a test.
How many did each child answer **correctly**?

(a)  I had 15 wrong.

(b) I had 12 wrong.

(c) I had 17 wrong.

2 (a) 86 – 15   (b) 99 – 17   (c) 83 – 11

(d) 69 – 14   (e) 75 – 12   (f) 78 – 18

3 (a) 49 – 16 = ■   **4** (a) 57 – ■ = 45

(b) 77 – 16 = ■   (b) 85 – ■ = 71

(c) 58 – 14 = ■   (c) ■ – 13 = 54

(d) 56 – 13 = ■   (d) ■ – 16 = 20

5

(a) 16 are broken.
How many are not broken?

(b) 14 are torn.
How many are not torn?

6 (a) Take 17 from 59.   (b) Subtract 15 from 97.

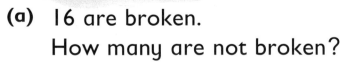

(c) 39 minus 19   (d) 25 take away 13

1 (a) 64 − 23   (b) 97 − 32   (c) 89 − 35
(d) 87 − 21   (e) 66 − 42   (f) 77 − 54

2 (a) 55 − 34   (b) 42 − 22   (c) 53 − 41
(d) 98 − 65   (e) 99 − 46   (f) 94 − 22

Javelin throws

Marco − 78 metres	Antony − 44 metres
Julius − 56 metres	Peter − 85 metres
Paul − 62 metres	Brutus − 33 metres

3 Find the difference in metres between the throws of
(a) Marco and Brutus   (b) Antony and Julius
(c) Julius and Marco   (d) Peter and Paul.

4 What is the difference between the **longest** and **shortest** throws?

5 (a) 57 − ■ = 32   (b) 85 − ■ = 41   (c) 77 − ■ = 54

Troy — 48 rowers
Juno — 35 rowers
Mars — 23 rowers
Rome — 79 rowers

1 Find the difference between the number of rowers in

  (a) *Troy* and *Juno*   **(b)** *Mars* and *Rome*.

2 How many more rowers are in *Rome* than in

  (a) *Troy*   **(b)** *Juno*?

3 How many fewer rowers are in *Mars* than in

  (a) *Juno*   **(b)** *Troy*?

4

- There are 99 Roman sailors altogether in the three galleys.
- There are 12 fewer sailors in the blue galley than in the green galley.
- There are 43 sailors in the green galley.

  How many sailors are in the
  (a) blue galley   **(b)** red galley?

1 How many are left?

(a) Eat 6. (b) Eat 7. (c) Eat 4.

 24  23  22

(d) Eat 5. (e) Eat 8. (f) Eat 9.

 21  27 25

2

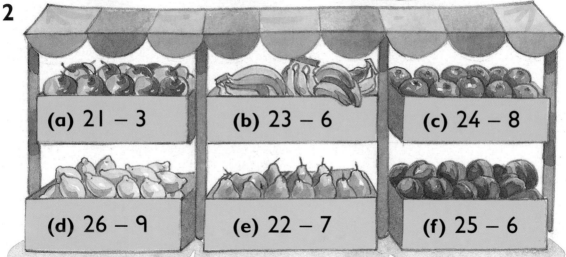

(a) 21 – 3 (b) 23 – 6 (c) 24 – 8

(d) 26 – 9 (e) 22 – 7 (f) 25 – 6

3 (a) 23 – 8 = ■ (b) 21 – 4 = ■ (c) 22 – 9 = ■

(d) 23 – ■ = 18 (e) 24 – ■ = 17 (f) 24 – ■ = 19

4 Which fruits cost 17p?

 22p 5p off apple

 26p 7p off pear

 25p 8p off lemon

1 How many are left?

(a) Buy 6. (b) Buy 4.

(33) (51)

(c) Buy 7. (d) Buy 9. (e) Buy 5.

(62) (30) (74)

2 (a) 72 – 3 (b) 54 – 6 (c) 60 – 8

(d) 81 – 2 (e) 95 – 9 (f) 32 – 8

3 (a) 84 – 6 = ■ (b) 92 – 4 = ■ (c) 50 – 7 = ■

(d) 71 – ■ = 69 (e) 82 – ■ = 78 (f) 34 – ■ = 29

4 Who will have 36 left?

Take away 8.

Subtract 5.

Subtract 7.

Lisa

Tom

Alex

(43) (45) (41)

29

1 Find the difference.

(a)

32   13

(b)

41   14

(c)

15   23

(d)

46   17

(e)

16   54

(f)

30   18

2 (a) 81 – 12   (b) 65 – 19   (c) 53 – 17

(d) 72 – 14   (e) 63 – 16   (f) 97 – 18

3 How many more flowers are red?

(a)

75   17

(b)

19   86

(c)

74   18

4 (a) 21 – ■ = 9   (b) 41 – ■ = 28   (c) 62 – ■ = 48

(d) ■ – 13 = 38   (e) ■ – 15 = 77   (f) ■ – 16 = 74

Subtraction to 100: teens numbers, bridging

HOME ACTIVITY 11

1 How many stickers are left?

(a) Give away 26.   (b) Give away 38.

(c) Give away 27.   (d) Give away 43.   (e) Give away 35.

2 (a) 77 – 39   (b) 92 – 64   (c) 68 – 29

    (d) 86 – 58   (e) 95 – 46   (f) 70 – 24

3 (a) How many more stickers has Eva than
                • Alan   • Babs?

I have 65.

I have 28.

(b) How many fewer stickers has Babs than Alan?

4 (a) 75 – ▧ = 57   (b) 67 – ▧ = 39   (c) 94 – ▧ = 56

    (d) ▧ – 47 = 35   (e) ▧ – 37 = 57   (f) ▧ – 36 = 36

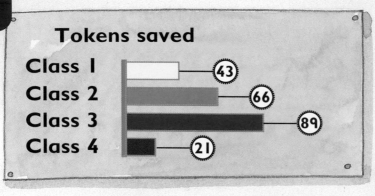

Tokens saved

Class 1   43
Class 2   66
Class 3   89
Class 4   21

1 How many more tokens has Class 3 than

   (a) Class 1   **(b)** Class 2   **(c)** Class 4?

2 What is the difference in tokens between

   (a) Class 2 and Class 4   **(b)** Class 4 and Class 1?

3 **(a)** 34 – 13   **(b)** 55 – 12   **(c)** 77 – 34

    (d) 98 – 85   **(e)** 76 – 46   **(f)** 88 – 53

    (g) 58 – 27   **(h)** 97 – 32   **(i)** 67 – 35

4 Class 3 has 89 tokens. They use 38.
   How many are left?

5 **(a)** 99 subtract 15

    (b) 75 minus 14

    (c) Take 62 from 96.

    (d) Subtract 17 from 69.

1 How many are left?

(a) Sell 28.

(b) Sell 37. (c) Sell 35. (d) Sell 53.

2 (a) 66 – 38   (b) 88 – 39   (c) 75 – 47

(d) 67 – 29   (e) 83 – 45   (f) 98 – 35

(g) 71 subtract 26   (h) Take 24 from 52.

3 How much more has Eva than

(a)  (b)

(c)  (d)

1 Copy and complete.

(a)

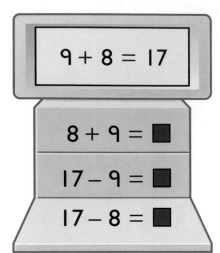

$9 + 8 = 17$

$8 + 9 = \blacksquare$

$17 - 9 = \blacksquare$

$17 - 8 = \blacksquare$

(b)

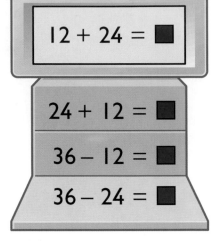

$12 + 24 = \blacksquare$

$24 + 12 = \blacksquare$

$36 - 12 = \blacksquare$

$36 - 24 = \blacksquare$

(c)

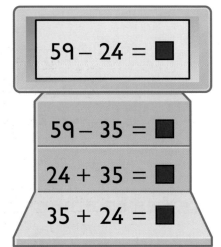

$59 - 24 = \blacksquare$

$59 - 35 = \blacksquare$

$24 + 35 = \blacksquare$

$35 + 24 = \blacksquare$

(d)

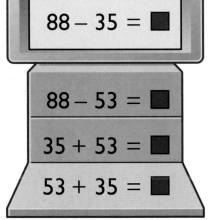

$88 - 35 = \blacksquare$

$88 - 53 = \blacksquare$

$35 + 53 = \blacksquare$

$53 + 35 = \blacksquare$

2 Use the addition fact.
Write two subtraction stories.

(a)  $11 + 7 = 18$

(b) $23 + 14 = 37$

(c)  $42 + 23 = 65$

(d)  $65 + 34 = 99$

1 Copy and complete.

(a)

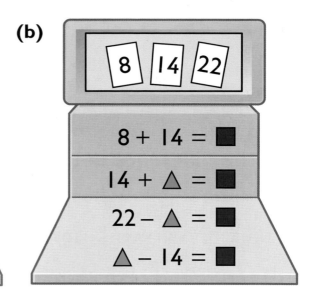

7 6 13

$7 + 6 = \blacksquare$

$6 + 7 = \blacksquare$

$13 - 6 = \blacksquare$

$13 - 7 = \blacksquare$

(b)

8 14 22

$8 + 14 = \blacksquare$

$14 + \triangle = \blacksquare$

$22 - \triangle = \blacksquare$

$\triangle - 14 = \blacksquare$

2 Write 4 number stories for each display.

(a)

6 9 15

(b)

12 9 21

(c)

8 19 27

(d)

33 28 5

3 Use the red number and **two** of the other numbers.
Write 4 number stories.

(a)

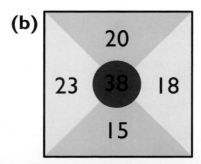

14
13 **25** 12
11

(b)

20
23 **38** 18
15

(c)

24
32 **50** 18
26

35

1 Find the difference between the numbers on the

(a) red and yellow buses

(b) brown and red buses

(c) blue and green buses

(d) yellow and brown buses

(e) brown and orange buses

(f) red and green buses.

2 (a) What kind of number is each answer in question 1?

(b) What kind of number is on each bus?

(c) What do you notice when you subtract an odd number from an odd number?

3 (a) The number on each of these buses

- is greater than 70
- is less than 100
- has a difference of 5 between its two digits.

What is the number on each bus?

(b) Which bus does each person drive?

My bus number is 22 less than Ena's.

1 For each person, find

(a) how much the tickets cost

(b) how much they have left.

15p 41p 25p

47p 32p 20p

Alan has 80p.

Beth has 68p.

Carlo has 75p.

Don has 96p.

Eric has 91p.

Fay has £1.

Amy

My 2 tickets cost 66p.

My 3 tickets cost 93p.

Ron

2 (a) What is the difference between the cost of Amy and Ron's tickets?

(b) Draw the tickets Amy and Ron bought.

1 Find the cost of two of each.

(a) 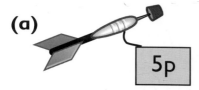 5p

(b)  8p

(c)  10p

2

(a) 2×3 (b) 2×0 (c) 2×7 (d) 4×2

(e) 9×2 (f) 2×1 (g) 2×2 (h) 6×2

(i) $2 \times \blacksquare = 14$ (j) $2 \times \blacksquare = 20$ (k) $2 \times \blacksquare = 8$

Two fives are ten and eight makes eighteen.

3 Find each child's score.

(a) Kate   (b) Zac   (c) Ben   (d) Zoe

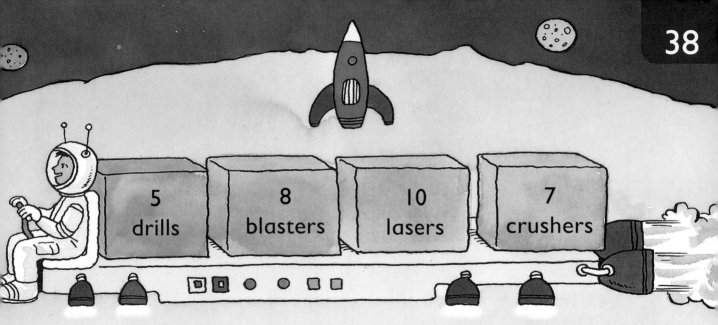

1 How many of these are carried on **ten** space buggies?

(a) drills   (b) blasters   (c) lasers   (d) crushers

2 (a) 10×4 (b) 9×10 (c) 10×0 (d) 10×6

     (e) 2×10 (f) 10×10 (g) 10×3 (h) 1×10

     (i) $10 \times \blacksquare = 70$ (j) $10 \times \blacksquare = 50$ (k) $10 \times \blacksquare = 90$

I am a Zonk

3 How many of these would **ten** Zonks have?

(a) (b) (c) (d) (e) (f)

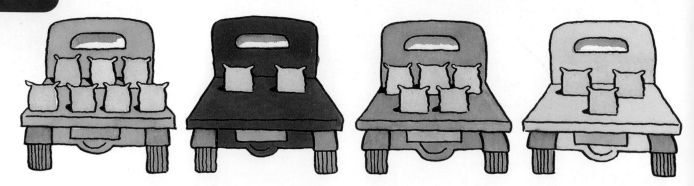

1 How many sacks are there on

(a) 5 green trucks (b) 5 red trucks (c) 10 blue trucks

(d) 5 yellow trucks (e) 6 blue trucks (f) 8 blue trucks

(g) 5 blue and 1 green truck (h) 4 blue and 5 red trucks?

2 How many wagons are pulled by

(a) 9 engines (b) 5 engines (c) 7 engines?

3 There are

(a) ■ helmets in 3 boxes

(b) ■ helmets in 8 boxes

(c) ■ helmets in 6 boxes

(d) ■ helmets in 4 boxes.

5
Safety Helmets

4 (a) $5 \times \blacksquare = 5$ (b) $5 \times \blacksquare = 0$ (c) $5 \times \blacksquare = 10$

(d) $\blacksquare \times 5 = 45$ (e) $\blacksquare \times 5 = 15$ (f) $\blacksquare \times 5 = 50$

1 How many

(a) red flowers in 3 baskets

(b) blue flowers in 7 baskets

(c) yellow flowers in 3 baskets

(d) blue flowers in 10 baskets

2

How many litres in 3 sacks of

(a) Plant Food   (b) Soil   (c) Bark   (d) Compost?

3 Plant Food is also sold in **7 litre** and **20 litre** sacks.

I have one 20 litre sack.

(a) Who has more Plant Food?

I have three 7 litre sacks.

(b) How much more?

(c) How many litres are there in three 20 litre sacks?

Jane   Ali

4 (a) $3 \times \blacksquare = 0$ (b) $3 \times \blacksquare = 12$ (c) $3 \times \blacksquare = 6$

(d) $\blacksquare \times 3 = 3$ (e) $\blacksquare \times 3 = 9$ (f) $\blacksquare \times 3 = 24$

(g) $3 \times \blacksquare = 15$ (h) $\blacksquare \times 3 = 27$ (i) $3 \times \blacksquare = 18$

BORO VALE F.C.

Match tickets

Adult £7 | Child £4 | Family £10

I How much does each have to pay?

(a) 4 Adult tickets please.

(b) 3 Child tickets please.

(c) 4 Family tickets please.

£8 | £9 | £4 | £6

2 What is the cost of

(a) 4

(b) 4

(c) 8

(d) 4

(e) 7  and I

(f) I and 4 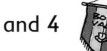 ?

3 (a) $4 \times \blacksquare = 24$

(b) $4 \times \blacksquare = 0$

(c) $4 \times \blacksquare = 4$

(d) $\blacksquare \times 4 = 20$

(e) $\blacksquare \times 4 = 36$

(f) $\blacksquare \times 4 = 40$

Each wagon has

water
6 barrels

flour
3 bags

beans
8 sacks

1 How many barrels of water are on

(a) 3 wagons   (b) 4 wagons   (c) 5 wagons?

2 How many bags of flour are on

(a) 4 wagons   (b) 7 wagons   (c) 9 wagons?

3 How many sacks of beans are on

(a) 3 wagons   (b) 4 wagons   (c) 5 wagons?

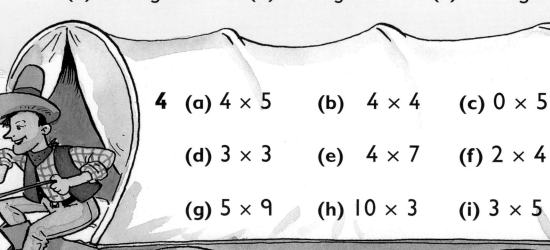

4 (a) 4×5 (b) 4×4 (c) 0×5

(d) 3×3 (e) 4×7 (f) 2×4

(g) 5×9 (h) 10×3 (i) 3×5

5 (a) $5 \times \blacksquare = 10$ (b) $7 \times \blacksquare = 35$ (c) $4 \times \blacksquare = 36$

(d) $\blacksquare \times 5 = 50$ (e) $\blacksquare \times 4 = 12$ (f) $\blacksquare \times 3 = 15$

43

TRADING POST

Shirts
10 dollars

Pots
4 dollars

Hats
8 dollars

Picks
3 dollars

Ropes
2 dollars

1 How many dollars does it cost to buy

(a) 4 pots   (b) 5 shirts   (c) 4 picks

(d) 3 hats   (e) 10 pots   (f) 5 hats

(g) 10 shirts   (h) 6 picks   (i) 9 ropes?

2 (a) 5×9 (b) 2×4 (c) 4×0

(d) 10×8 (e) 5×3 (f) 7×10

3 How many candles are in

(a) 2 boxes   (b) 4 boxes?

4 How many biscuits are in

(a) 5 tins   (b) 10 tins?

8 candles

6
biscuits

5 (a) $2 \times \blacksquare = 14$ (b) $3 \times \blacksquare = 30$ (c) $10 \times \blacksquare = 40$

(d) $\blacksquare \times 5 = 25$ (e) $\blacksquare \times 2 = 12$ (f) $\blacksquare \times 10 = 0$

 40  20  30  50

1 How many

(a) in 2 boxes

(b) in 3 boxes

(c)  in 5 boxes

(d) in 4 boxes

(e) 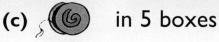 in 4 boxes

(f)  in 10 boxes?

2 (a) twice 30   (b) 3 times 20   (c) double 50

(d) 20 multiplied by 10   (e) multiply 50 by 5

3 (a) 3 × 40   (b) 10 × 30   (c) 4 × 20

(d) 30 × 3   (e) 40 × 5   (f) 50 × 10

4 How many

(a) balloons are in 2 packets

(b) beads are in 5 packets

(c) marbles are in 4 packets?

20 balloons   30 beads   40 marbles

rhino

21p

44p

elephant

snake

32p

13p

23p

lion

crocodile

1 **Find the cost of these models.**

(a) 2 rhinos   (b) 2 snakes   (c) 2 lions

(d) 2 crocodiles   (e) 2 elephants   (f) 3 snakes

(g) 3 lions   (h) 3 crocodiles   (i) 4 rhinos

2 (a) 2×33 (b) 2×42 (c) 3×31

     (d) 3×22 (e) 5×11 (f) 2×43

     (g) 2×35 (h) 4×22 (i) 3×33

3 **How many models are in**

(a) 3 sets of farm animals

(b) 2 sets of dinosaurs

(c) 3 sets of zoo animals?

12
farm animals

21
zoo
animals

25
dinosaurs

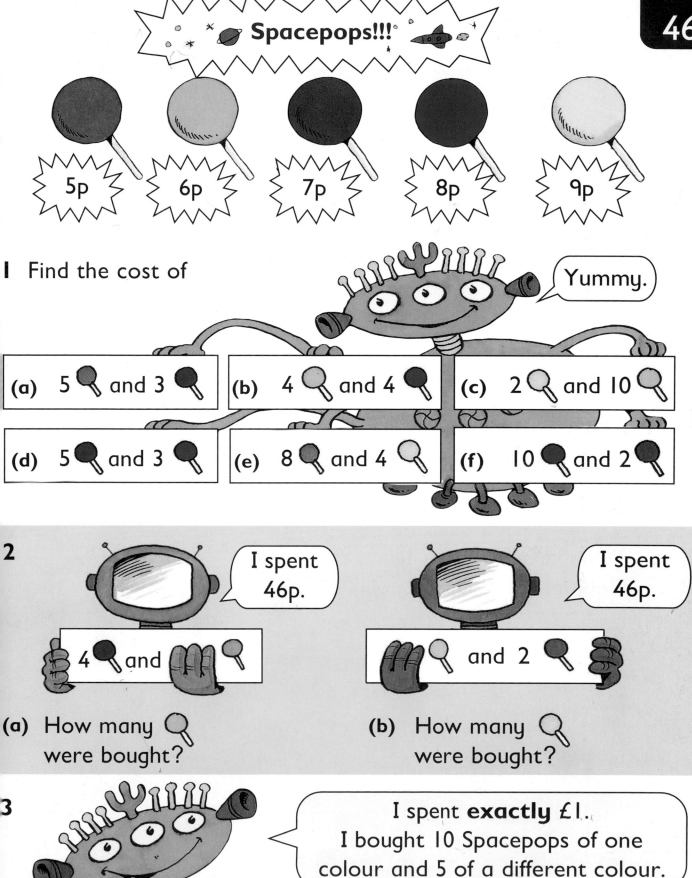

Spacepops!!!

5p   6p   7p   8p   9p

1 Find the cost of

Yummy.

(a) 5 and 3

(b) 4 and 4

(c) 2 and 10

(d) 5 and 3

(e) 8 and 4

(f) 10 and 2

2

I spent 46p.

I spent 46p.

4 and

and 2

(a) How many were bought?

(b) How many were bought?

3 I spent **exactly** £1.
I bought 10 Spacepops of one colour and 5 of a different colour.

Which **two** colours of Spacepops did the Zonk buy?

TOPIC ASSESSMENT   Multiplication: using and applying

1 Share equally between 2 people.

(a)

8 tickets

(b)

20 posters

(c)

12 T-shirts

(d)

16 badges

2 Divide.

    (a) $4 \div 2$ (b) $14 \div 2$ (c) $2 \div 2$

    (d) $6 \div 2$ (e) $0 \div 2$ (f) $18 \div 2$

3 There are 10 tickets left.
How many people can buy 2 each?

4

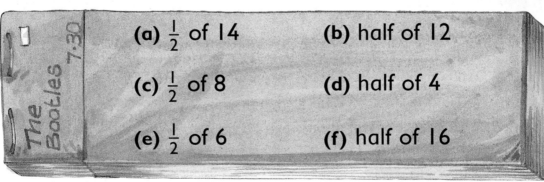

(a) $\frac{1}{2}$ of 14   (b) half of 12

(c) $\frac{1}{2}$ of 8   (d) half of 4

(e) $\frac{1}{2}$ of 6   (f) half of 16

5 (a) $\frac{1}{2}$ of ■ $= 5$ (b) $\frac{1}{2}$ of ■ $= 1$ (c) $\frac{1}{2}$ of ■ $= 10$

    (d) half of ■ $= 9$ (e) half of ■ $= 0$ (f) half of ■ $= 7$

1 There are 10 seats in each row.
How many rows can be made with

(a) 30 seats   (b) 80 seats   (c) 50 seats?

2

(a) $70 \div 10 = \blacksquare$

(b) $20 \div 10 = \blacksquare$

(c) $10 \div 10 = \blacksquare$

(d) $90 \div 10 = \blacksquare$

3

(a) $40 \div 10 = \blacksquare$

(b) $100 \div 10 = \blacksquare$

(c) $0 \div 10 = \blacksquare$

(d) $60 \div 10 = \blacksquare$

4 (a) Divide 20 by 10.   (b) Share 30 equally among 10.

(c) 70 divided by 10   (d) 100 divided by 10

(e) Divide 0 by 10.   (f) How many tens make 80?

5 How many groups of 10?

(a)   50 CDs   (b)   40 caps

6 (a) $\blacksquare \div 10 = 6$ (b) $\blacksquare \div 10 = 1$ (c) $\blacksquare \div 10 = 9$

1 How many groups of 5 links are there in a chain with

        (a) 45 links   **(b)** 30 links

        (c) 35 links   **(d)** 50 links?

2 **(a)** $20 \div 5$ **(b)** $40 \div 5$ **(c)** $0 \div 5$

    (d) $50 \div 5$ **(e)** $25 \div 5$ **(f)** $35 \div 5$

3 Share equally among 5 party bags.

      (a) 15   **(b)** 40

      (c) 5   **(d)** 10

4 **(a)** Divide 45 by 5.   **(b)** Share 15 equally among 5.

    (c) 30 divided by 5   **(d)** 20 shared equally among 5

    (e) How many fives make 25?

5

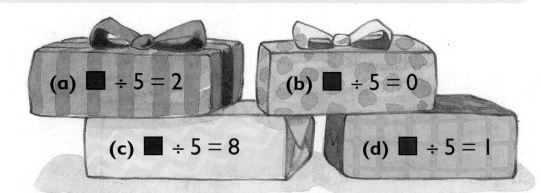

    (a) $\blacksquare \div 5 = 2$ **(b)** $\blacksquare \div 5 = 0$

    (c) $\blacksquare \div 5 = 8$ **(d)** $\blacksquare \div 5 = 1$

1
 (a) 5 ÷ 5    (b) 45 ÷ 5   (c) 10 ÷ 5    (d) 50 ÷ 5

2 Prizes are sold in packs of 5.
How many packs are used for

(a) 40   (b) 10   (c) 25

(d) 15   (e) 5   (f) 30   ?

3 Share equally among 5 plates.

(a) 25   (b) 50

(c) 35   (d) 20

4 (a) ■ ÷ 5 = 9   (b) ■ ÷ 5 = 3   (c) ■ ÷ 5 = 6

(d) ■ ÷ 5 = 0   (e) ■ ÷ 5 = 7   (f) ■ ÷ 5 = 4

1 Share equally among 3 rugs.

(a)  30

(b)  18

(c)  24

2 How many children can have 3 each?

(a)  6

(b)  15

(c)  9

(d) 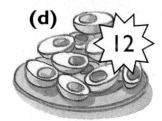 12

(e)  27

(f)  21

3 Copy and complete.

$0 \div 3 = \blacksquare$
$3 \div 3 = \blacksquare$
$6 \div 3 = \blacksquare$
$9 \div 3 = \blacksquare$

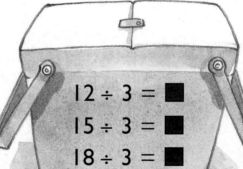

$12 \div 3 = \blacksquare$
$15 \div 3 = \blacksquare$
$18 \div 3 = \blacksquare$

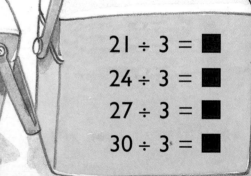

$21 \div 3 = \blacksquare$
$24 \div 3 = \blacksquare$
$27 \div 3 = \blacksquare$
$30 \div 3 = \blacksquare$

I Divide equally among 3 children.

(a)  6

(b)  3

(c)  18

(d)  24

(e)  12

(f) 30

2 How many teams of 3?

(a) 9 boys   (b) 27 girls

(c) 15 children   (d) 21 children

3 (a) Divide 6 by 3.   (b) Share 18 equally among 3.

(c) 12 divided by 3   (d) How many threes make 27?

4 There were 26 sausages.
Patch stole 2.
Divide the rest of the sausages
equally among 3 plates.

5 (a) $\blacksquare \div 3 = 5$ (b) $\blacksquare \div 3 = 1$ (c) $\blacksquare \div 3 = 10$

(d) $\blacksquare \div 3 = 3$ (e) $\blacksquare \div 3 = 7$ (f) $\blacksquare \div 3 = 0$

1 Put four wheels on each car. How many can now race?

(a)

12

(b)

20

(c)

40

(d)

32

(e)

16

(f)

28

2 (a) $8 \div 4$ (b) $36 \div 4$ (c) $24 \div 4$

    (d) $0 \div 4$ (e) $20 \div 4$ (f) $16 \div 4$

3 (a) 4 divided by 4   (b) One quarter of 28

    (c) Divide 40 by 4.   (d) How many fours make 32?

    (e) One quarter of 12   (f) Divide 8 by 4.

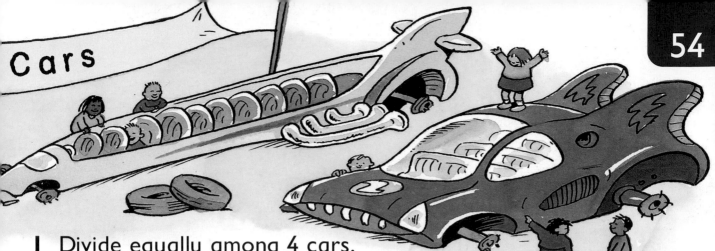

Cars

1 Divide equally among 4 cars.

(a)  36

(b)  20

(c)  8

(d)  24

(e)  16

(f)  4

2 **(a)** $12 \div 4$ **(b)** $32 \div 4$ **(c)** $40 \div 4$

3 **(a)** $\blacksquare \div 4 = 6$ **(b)** $\blacksquare \div 4 = 2$ **(c)** $\blacksquare \div 4 = 0$

   (d) $\blacksquare \div 4 = 5$ **(e)** $\blacksquare \div 4 = 7$ **(f)** $\blacksquare \div 4 = 1$

4 Follow the track. →
   Which car wins the race?

40	÷	4	=	■
=	■	−	4	+
10	=	■	=	6
×	4	÷	■	=
■	=	4	÷	■

1 How many teams?

(a) 10 girls in teams of 2   (b) 12 boys in teams of 3

(c) 20 boys in teams of 5   (d) 50 girls in teams of 10

(e) 27 children in teams of 3   (f) 24 children in teams of 4

2 Share equally among the teams.

(a) 8 ropes ⟶ | 4 teams | (b) 10 benches ⟶ | 10 teams |

(c) 45 hoops ⟶ | 5 teams | (d) 16 skittles ⟶ | 2 teams |

(e) 40 balls ⟶ | 4 teams | (f) 70 bean bags ⟶ | 10 teams |

3 Find each number.

(a) 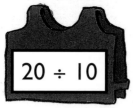 $30 \div 5$

(b)  $6 \div 3$

(c) 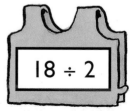 $18 \div 2$

(d)  $20 \div 10$

(e) 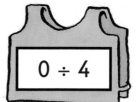 $0 \div 4$

(f)  $24 \div 3$

4 How many balls?

?

There are less than 25 balls

I can share them equally among three teams **or** four teams.

1 Divide equally among the children.

(a) 40 throws, 5 children

(b) 16 throws, 4 children

(c) 90 skips, 10 children

(d) 18 serves, 3 children

(e) 8 catches, 2 children

(f)   50 hits, 5 teams

2 (a) ■ ÷ 10 = 8   (b) ■ ÷ 4 = 9   (c) ■ ÷ 3 = 2

(d) ■ ÷ 5 = 1   (e) ■ ÷ 2 = 0   (f) ■ ÷ 10 = 3

3 (a) Divide 28 by 4.   (b) Share 30 equally among 3.

(c) 40 divided by 10   (d) How many groups of 5 in 10?

(e) Divide 21 by 3.   (f) How many fours make 12?

(g) Half of 14   (h) One quarter of 32

4 (a) Half of the ropes are long.
How many ropes are long?

12 ropes

(b) Half of the long ropes are red.
How many of the long ropes are red?

(c) What fraction of **all** the ropes are long **and** red?

1 **(a)** double 12

(c) double 16

(e) double 20

(b) half of 24

(d) half of 32

(f) half of 40

2 **(a)** half of 36

(d) $\frac{1}{2}$ of 22

(b) half of 28

(e) $\frac{1}{2}$ of 30

(c) half of 34

(f) $\frac{1}{2}$ of 26

3

(a) 25 multiplied by 2

(b) half of 50

(c) $\frac{1}{2}$ of 70

(d) half of 80

(e) $\frac{1}{2}$ of 100

4 **(a)** Half of 200

(c) Double 200

(e) Half of 500

(g) $\frac{1}{2}$ of 1000

(b) Divide 600 by 2.

(d) 300 divided by 2

(f) Divide 700 by 2.

(h) Twice 450

Copy and complete.

(a)

$4 \times 5 = 20$

$5 \times 4 = \blacksquare$

$20 \div 4 = \blacksquare$

$20 \div 5 = \blacksquare$

(b)

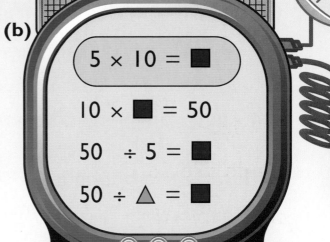

$5 \times 10 = \blacksquare$

$10 \times \blacksquare = 50$

$50 \div 5 = \blacksquare$

$50 \div \triangle = \blacksquare$

(c)

$6 \div 2 = 3$

$6 \div \blacksquare = 2$

$2 \times 3 = \blacksquare$

$3 \times \triangle = \blacksquare$

(d)

$15 \div 3 = \blacksquare$

$15 \div \triangle = \blacksquare$

$3 \times \blacksquare = 15$

$\triangle \times 3 = \blacksquare$

Use the multiplication fact. Write two division stories.

(a) $10 \times 2 = 20$ **(b)** $3 \times 4 = 12$ **(c)** $4 \times 2 = 8$

Write 4 number stories each time.

(a) 2 5 10   **(b)** 40 4 10

1 Divide 19 children equally among 4 mats.

   (a) How many children are on each mat?

   (b) How many are left over?

2 Find each answer and remainder.

   (a) Divide the beanbags
   equally among 4 teams.

23 beanbags

   (b) Share the hoops
   equally among 5 teams.

29 hoops

3 (a) How many teams can each have 10 balls?

   (b) How many balls are left over?

89 balls

4 Which number am I?

| 17 | 14 | 16 | 23 |

   (a) Divide me by 10 and my remainder is 7.

   (b) When divided by 5 my remainder is 3.

   (c) Divide me by 3 or by 4
   and my remainder is 2.

5 Write a remainder clue for 29 .

1 There are 27 children.

   (a) How many teams of 4 can be made?

   (b) No more than 4 children can sit at a table. How many tables are needed?

2  Each child must have 10 cards. How many children can play?

3 How many pairs of dice?

4  The dominoes are shared equally among 5 players.

   How many dominoes does each player have?

5 Each shelf can hold 3 jigsaws.

   How many shelves are needed to hold 25 jigsaws?

1 How much?

(a)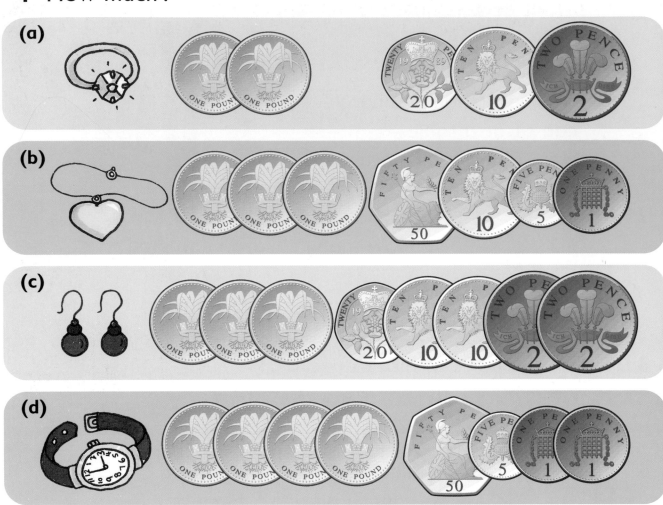

(b)

(c)

(d)

2 Who has more money?

Bob

Sally

3 Lay out coins to buy each item. List the coins.

(a)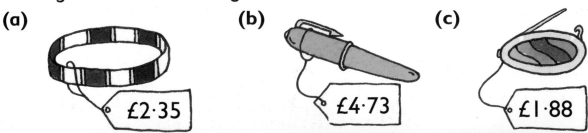

£2·35

(b)

£4·73

(c)

£1·88

1 How many of each coin to make £2?

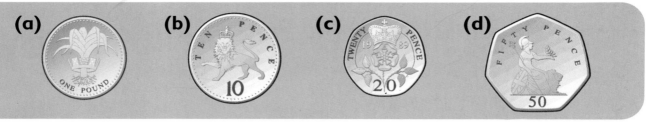

(a)   (b)   (c)   (d)

2 How much?

(a)

(b)

3 List coins to buy each item. Use as few coins as possible.

(a) £2·80   (b) £5·43   (c) £9·65   (d) £7·98

4 Which item is the **(a)** most expensive **(b)** least expensive?

5 Choose from these coins. List four **different** ways of making £5.

David has saved **£1·34**.

1 Write each amount in **pounds and pence**.

(a)

392p

(b)
657p

(c)
405p

(d) 213p   **(e)** 860p   **(f)** 442p   **(g)** 131p

(h) 950p   **(i)** 728p   **(j)** 504p   **(k)** 96p

2 Write each amount in **pence**.

(a) £2·48   **(b)** £5·04   **(c)** £0·57

(d) £9·35   **(e)** £3·61   **(f)** £1·53   **(g)** £6·29

(h) £5·70   **(i)** £8·06   **(j)** £7·90   **(k)** £4·00

3

£2·83   £4·65   238p   564p

Which bank has **(a)** most money **(b)** least money?

1 List the coins in your change from **£1** when you buy

(a) 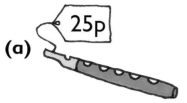 25p

(b) 63p

(c) 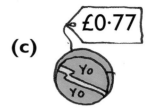 £0·77 .

2 List the coins in your change from **£2** when you buy

(a)  £1·32

(b)  £1·05

(c)  86p .

3 How much does each child have left?

(a) 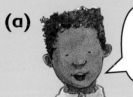 I had £2. I spent £1·40

(b)  I had £4. I spent £2·50

(c)  I had £1. I spent 49p

4 How much does each of these children have left?

(a) Greg had  . He spent 90p.

(b) Ray had  . He spent £2·80.

5 Suzy bought a toy. She paid with a £2 coin.

Her change was

How much did she spend?

1 Find how much money each child has.

Tim

Zoe

Mia

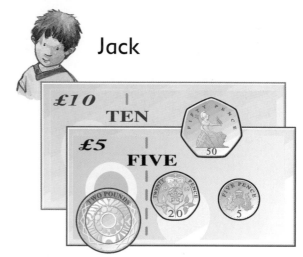

Jack

2 Lay out and list notes and coins to buy each item.

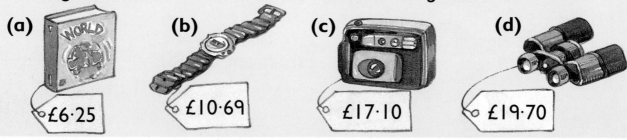

(a) WORLD £6·25

(b) £10·69

(c) £17·10

(d) £19·70

3 Write an amount which is more than the price of the

 but less than the price of the  .

1 How much money does each child have?

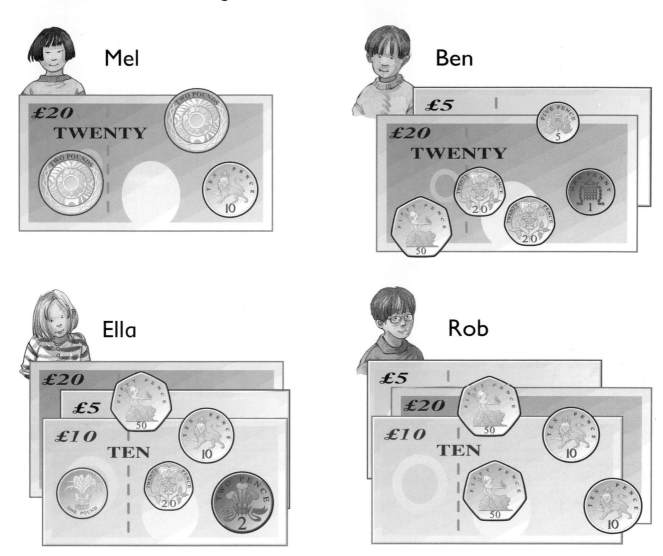

Mel

Ben

Ella

Rob

2 Lay out and list notes and coins to buy each item.

(a) £22·30

(b) £26·55

(c) £30·62

(d) £35·90

1 List the coins in each child's change.

(a) £5 £3·50

(b) £5 £2·30

(c) £10 £6·90

(d) £10 £7·60

(e) £5 £2·75

(f) £10 £8·20

£0·40	£1·20	£0·70	£0·90	£2·30	£1·50

2 Find the total cost of a

(a) ball and badge   (b) doll and pen   (c) ball and doll

(d) truck and doll   (e) pen and badge   (f) flag and badge.

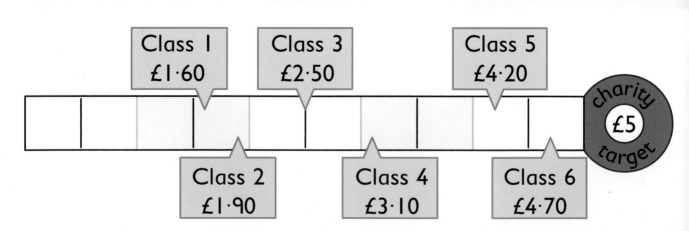

Class 1 £1·60

Class 2 £1·90

Class 3 £2·50

Class 4 £3·10

Class 5 £4·20

Class 6 £4·70

charity £5 target

3 How much money does each class still need to collect?

1 Find the cost of each order for comics.

Comic	Copies
(a) Wizzo	2
(b) Pop week	3
(c) Monster	4
(d) Footie	10

2 For how many weeks must each child save to buy the diary?

Diary £3

(a) Meg   I save 30p a week.

(b) Ravi   I save 20p a week.

(c) Lena   I save 15p a week.

3

Notes 51p

Gaby bought 6 note pads.
How much was her change from £4?

4 Find the cost of each of these books.

- Pay for the brown book with a £1 coin.
  Your change is 10p.

- The blue and brown books together cost £4·90.

- The blue book costs £1·20 more than the green book.

- The green book costs twice as much as the red book.

- The brown book is 50p cheaper than the red book.

1 List **five** coins to make

    (a) 74p   **(b)** 66p   **(c)** £1·27   **(d)** £2·61

2 Paul and Salma each have five **different** coins.

    (a) What amount does each have?

    (b) List other sets of five different coins and the amounts they make.

Paul

Salma

3

Burger £2·20   Pizza £3·50   Fish £3·90

Curry £4·30   Salad £1·10   Chicken £8·80

(a) Which **two** meals can be bought for **exactly £5**?

(b) Which **three** meals can be bought for **exactly £10**?

(c) Which meals can be bought for **exactly £6·50**?

(d) How much is your change from £10 when you buy Salad **and** Chicken?

1 What fraction of each shape is red?

(a)

(b)

(c)

(d)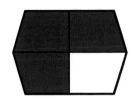

(e)

(f)

2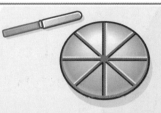

apple   plum   cherry   pear

Anna buys one half of each pie.
How many **pieces** of each pie does she buy?

3 (a) one half of 22   (b) one quarter of 20

(c) one half of 24   (d) one quarter of 36

(e) $\frac{1}{2}$ of 30   (f) $\frac{1}{4}$ of 32   (g) $\frac{1}{2}$ of 26   (h) $\frac{1}{4}$ of 28

4 Find
(a) one half of 40
(b) one quarter of 40
(c) three quarters of 40

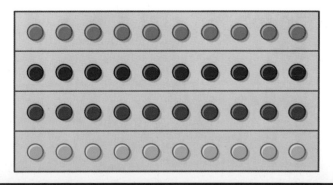

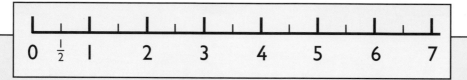 $1\frac{1}{2}$ circles are coloured.

1 How many of these circles are coloured?

(a)

(b)

(c)

(d)

(e)

(f)

2 Count in halves. Write down each number

(a) from 0 to 3

(b) from 2 to 5

(c) from 7 to 4

(d) from 4 to 1.

3 Which children are correct?

One half is greater than one quarter.

Three quarters is less than one half.

Three quarters is greater than one half.

Liam

 Ali

 Jill

1 **(a)** Divide each tray of rings equally among 10 people.

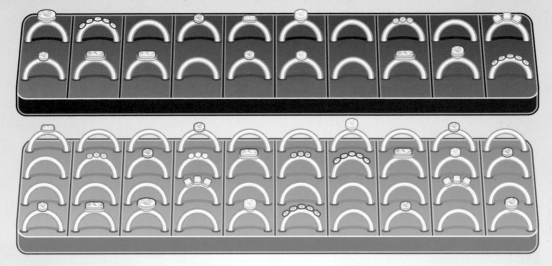

(b) Find one tenth of the rings on each tray.

(c) What do you notice when you

divide by 10   and   find one tenth?

2 **(a)** one tenth of 30   **(b)** $\frac{1}{10}$ of 90   **(c)** one tenth of 10

   (d) $\frac{1}{10}$ of 50   **(e)** one tenth of 70   **(f)** $\frac{1}{10}$ of 100

3 What fraction of the pattern on the box is

   (a) blue   **(b)** green   **(c)** not coloured?

4 There are 80 jewels in the box.
   One tenth of them are diamonds.
   How many are **not** diamonds?

1

Double each number.

(a) 12   (b) 15   (c) 18   (d) 19   (e) 50

(f) 30   (g) 35   (h) 20   (i) 45   (j) 100

2 Write each number from the blue box with its double from the red box.

60	70	85
55	95	90
65	75	80

150	130	110
160	170	180
190	140	120

3

(a) 24 + 25	25 + 25 = 50	(b) 25 + 26
(c) 15 + 17	17 + 17 = 34	(d) 17 + 19

(e) 14 + 15   (f) 35 + 36   (g) 16 + 14   (h) 50 + 52

4

(a) 80 + 90	90 + 90 = 180	(b) 90 + 100
(c) 55 + 60	60 + 60 = 120	(d) 60 + 65

(e) 70 + 80   (f) 50 + 60   (g) 45 + 50   (h) 95 + 100

1 Add the numbers on the
   (a) red jars   **(b)** blue jars   **(c)** green jars.

90   70   80   20   50   60

2

(a) 90 + 70   (b) 40 + 80   (c) 50 + 90

(d) 30 + ■ = 120   (e) ■ + 60 = 130   (f) 70 + ■ = 110

3 Find each total.

(a)  10 91

(b)  50 74

(c)  81 40

(d)  36 70

(e)  98 10

(f)  80 49

4

   (a) 50 + 83   (b) 42 + 60   (c) 35 + 90

   (d) 70 + 57   (e) 40 + 48   (f) 66 + 80

5   (a) 84 + ■ = 104   (b) ■ + 99 = 139

1 How many letters altogether?

(a)

52   67

(b)

34   74

(c)

61   85

2 Who has more stamps?

I have 61 and 81.

Cal

I have 77 and 63.

Lori

3 Find each total.

(a)

28   83

(b)

57   65

(c)

46   96

4

(a) 43 + 94   (b) 82 + 25   (c) 39 + 71

(d) 66 + 53   (e) 78 + 58   (f) 33 + 79

(g) 87 + 47   (h) 24 + 97   (i) 57 + 86

1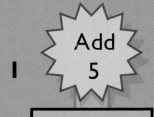

Add 5

| (a) 323 |
| (b) 404 |
| (c) 555 |

2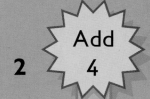

Add 4

| (a) 152 |
| (b) 135 |
| (c) 314 |

3

Add 6

| (a) 411 |
| (b) 500 |
| (c) 244 |

4

(a) 201 plus 8

(b) 842 add 7

(c) 111 + 9

(d) Add 3 to 756.

(e) What is the sum of 423 and 7?

5

(a) 327 + 5

(b) 149 plus 8

(c) 216 add 6

6

(a) Add 4 to 419.

(b) 526 + 7

(c) 3 plus 608

7

(a) 215 add 10

(b) What is the sum of 153 and 8?

(c) How many do 10 and 536 make altogether?

(d) 6 + 498

(e) What is the total of 299 and 7?

1

(a) 347 + 9   347 + 10 = 357   (b) 347 + 11

(c) 263 + 9   (d) 263 + 11

(e) 415 + 9   (f) 415 + 11

(g) 606 + 9   (h) 893 + 11

(i) 724 + 9   (j) 758 + 11

(k) 692 + 9   (l) 279 + 11

2 152 knights in a castle.
9 more ride in.
How many now?

I have 11 more coins than Stan.

I have 9 more coins than Stan.

Ralf   Stan   Max

508 coins

3 How many coins does each king have?

1 Add the **(a)** red numbers   **(b)** green numbers
         (c) yellow numbers   **(d)** blue numbers.

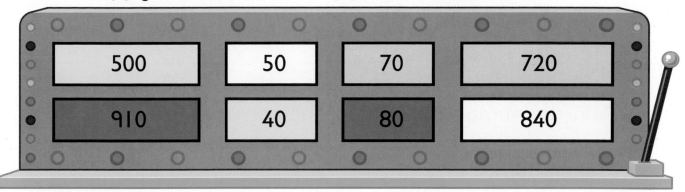

500	50	70	720
910	40	80	840

2

(a) 340 add 30   **(b)** 230 + 60   **(c)** 50 plus 450

(d) Add 60 to 720.   **(e)** Find the sum of 660 and 40.

3 Write the missing numbers.

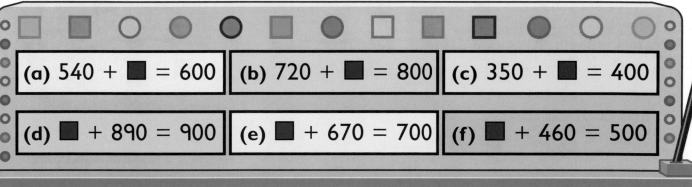

(a) $540 + \blacksquare = 600$ **(b)** $720 + \blacksquare = 800$ **(c)** $350 + \blacksquare = 400$

(d) $\blacksquare + 890 = 900$ **(e)** $\blacksquare + 670 = 700$ **(f)** $\blacksquare + 460 = 500$

4

(a) 227 + 60   **(b)** 308 + 30   **(c)** 70 + 529

(d) 80 + 117   **(e)** 222 + 20   **(f)** 104 + 90

(g) Add 40 and 347.   **(h)** 636 plus 50

1 Add the numbers on tins of the **same colour**.

2 Make 1000.

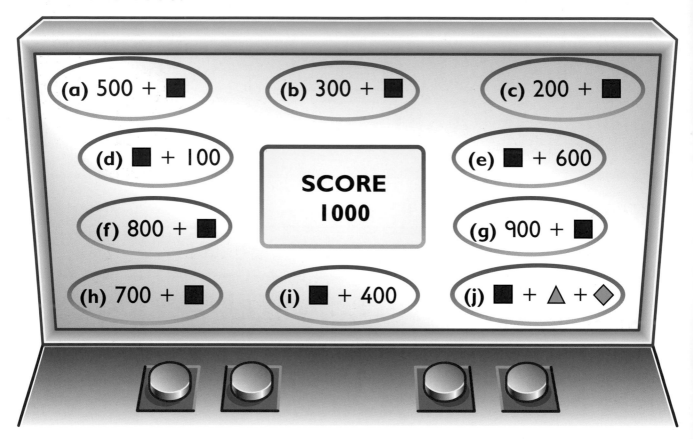

(a) 500 + ■

(b) 300 + ■

(c) 200 + ■

(d) ■ + 100

(e) ■ + 600

SCORE 1000

(f) 800 + ■

(g) 900 + ■

(h) 700 + ■

(i) ■ + 400

(j) ■ + △ + ◇

3 (a) 300 + 47

(b) 11 + 100

(c) 900 + 99

(d) 400 + 145

(e) 386 + 500

(f) 202 + 200

(g) 600 + 237

(h) 491 + 400

(i) 188 + 800

4 (a) 57 + ■ = 857

(b) 400 + ■ = 909

(c) ■ + 155 = 555

Barton School

303 children

Elmwood Village School

24 children

Doon Valley School

42 children

Penworth School

225 children

1 How many children altogether attend

(a) Barton and Elmwood

(b) Doon Valley and Penworth

(c) Barton and Doon Valley

(d) Penworth and Elmwood

(e) Elmwood, Barton and Doon Valley?

2 16 new children join Barton.
How many children are there now?

3 **(a)** 416 + 63   **(b)** 44 + 131   **(c)** 701 + 98

(d) 222 + 22   **(e)** 73 + 925   **(f)** 812 + 81

(g) 345 + 200 + 42   **(h)** 230 + 21 + 5

1 105 runners.
10 drop out.
How many are left?

2 Subtract 10 from

(a) 303   (b) 501   (c) 604   (d) 400

(e) 708   (f) 910   (g) 202   (h) 809

3 137 spectators. 40 go home.
How many are left?

4 (a) 126 − 30   (b) 150 − 70   (c) 131 − 60

(d) 110 − 20   (e) 166 − 80   (f) 105 − 90

5 (a) 120 − ■ = 40   (b) 114 − ■ = 94

1

(a) 258 – 9

258 – 10 = 248

(b) 258 – 11

(c) 325 – 9

(d) 325 – 11

(e) 402 – 9

(f) 402 – 11

(g) 333 – 9

(h) 217 – 11

(i) 200 – 9

(j) 500 – 11

2 (a) 194
9 are caught.
How many are left?

(b) 126
11 fly away.
How many are left?

My rod cost
£9 less than Sue's.

My rod
cost £107.

Sue's rod cost £11
more than mine.

Tim

Sue

Ann

3 What was the cost of **(a)** Tim's rod **(b)** Ann's rod?

bike
£200

Hi-Fi
£400

TV
£700

computer
£500

1 How much **more** does the computer cost than
(a) the bike   (b) the Hi-Fi?

2 How much **cheaper** than the TV is
(a) the computer   (b) the Hi-Fi?   (c) the bike?

3 (a) 900 – 600   (b) 300 – 100   (c) 800 – 700

I have
£409.

only £100

I have
£573.

Pam

Rod

4 Pam and Rod both buy a video.
How much does each have left?

5 (a) 727 – 300   (b) 399 – 200   (c) 940 – 600

(d) 844 – 400   (e) 706 – 500   (f) 112 – 100

6 (a) 900 – ■ = 200   (b) ■ – 100 = 385

(c) ■ – 700 = 237   (c) 586 – ■ = 186

1 (a) How many centimetres **taller** than Ray is Meg?

(b) How many centimetres **shorter** than Li is Jo?

2 What is the difference in height between
(a) Ray and Li?   (b) Jo and Meg?

3 (a) 262 − 258   (b) 593 − 587   (c) 725 − 719

(d) 312 − 309   (e) 471 − 466   (f) 650 − 644

4 What is the difference in height between
(a) the Tower and the Hotel   (b) the Hall and the Centre
(c) the Centre and the Hotel   (d) the Hall and the Tower?

5 (a) 303 − 296   (b) 401 − 395   (c) 503 − 499

(d) 903 − 898   (e) 602 − 594   (f) 700 − 693

6 (a) 563 − ■ = 556   (b) 806 − ■ = 798   (c) ■ − 4 = 299

**Upper Stand
500 seats**

**Lower Stand
304 seats**

1 How many seats are there altogether in the Stand?

There are only 60 tickets left for the Upper Stand.

I have sold 299 tickets for the Lower Stand.

2 How many tickets **(a)** for the Upper Stand have been sold

(b) for the Lower Stand are left?

3 200 Lower Stand tickets have been sold to **adults**. How many have been sold to **children**?

My programme is number **160**.

My programme number is **11** less than Ian's.

Ian's number is **double** mine.

Ian

Ann

Sam

4 What programme number has **(a)** Ann **(b)** Sam?

5 Find the winning Lucky Dip number.

6 less than 503 minus the sum of 230 and 70

1 Use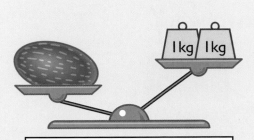
How many maths textbooks altogether weigh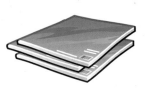
(a) about 1 kg   (b) about $\frac{1}{2}$ kg?

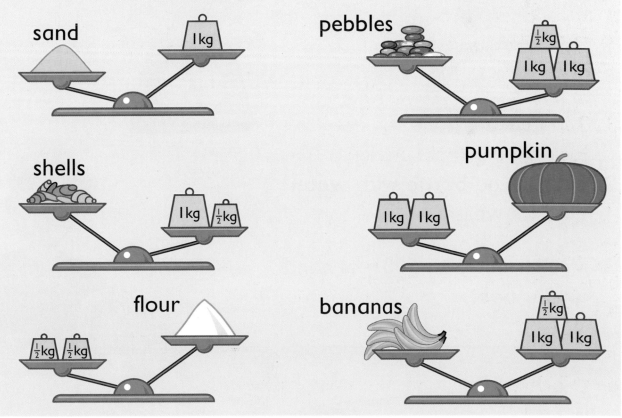

The melon weighs more than 2 kg.

The tin weighs less than $1\frac{1}{2}$ kg.

2 Write about the weight of each of these items.

sand

pebbles

shells

pumpkin

flour

bananas

3 Find an object which you estimate weighs between 2 kg and 3 kg.

The rice weighs about

$2\frac{1}{2}$ kg   or   2kg 500g

Rice

1 Write each of these weights in two ways.

(a)

(b)

(c)

(d)

2 Fill a large bottle with water.
Find its weight.

3 Weigh out 1 kg 500 g of sand
into a box.

1 Which items weigh
   (a) more than $\frac{1}{2}$ kg   (b) less than $\frac{1}{2}$ kg?

2 Which **two** items together weigh
   (a) $\frac{1}{2}$ kg   (b) 1 kg?   (c) $1\frac{1}{2}$ kg?

3 Which **three** items together weigh 1 kg?

4 Match each item to its weight.

500 g	30 kg
100 g	3 kg

5 Choose the weight for each item.

(a) | 100 g | 1 kg | 20 kg | 200 kg |

(b)  | 300 g | 3 kg | 30 kg | 300 kg |

Use a half metre strip.

1 Measure these lengths. Label them as

| shorter than $\frac{1}{2}$ metre | **or** | longer than $\frac{1}{2}$ metre |

(a)    **(b)** 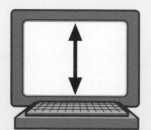   **(c)**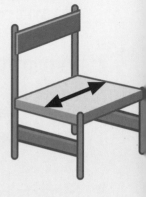

2 Find two objects
   (a) each about $\frac{1}{2}$ m long   **(b)** with lengths longer than $\frac{1}{2}$ m but shorter than 1 m.

The bench is about $2\frac{1}{2}$ metres long.

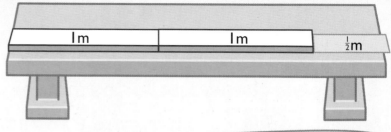

3 Use metre sticks and half metre strips to measure some objects.

object	length
bench	about $2\frac{1}{2}$ m
desk	
bookcase	
table	

1 metre   10 20 30 40 50 60 70 80 90

The rope is about 1m 70 cm long.

1 Estimate then measure.

32+17
84+29

100+350
250+120

(a) width of the board

(b) length of 5 maths books

(c) your height   **(d)** a friend's height

(e) width of a door

(f) length of a floor mat

2 Find two objects which you **estimate** are longer than 3 metres. Measure to check.

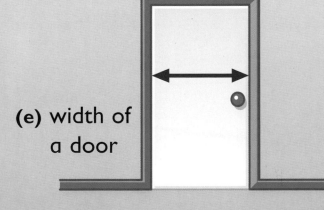

1 Find the length of each object.

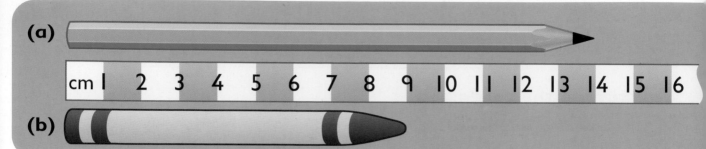

(a)

cm 1 2 3 4 5 6 7 8 9 10 11 12 13 14 15 16

(b)

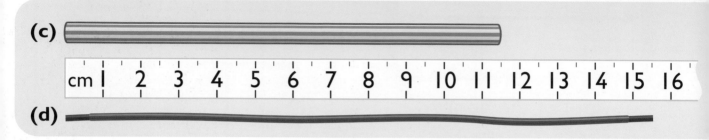

(c)

cm 1 2 3 4 5 6 7 8 9 10 11 12 13 14 15 16

(d)

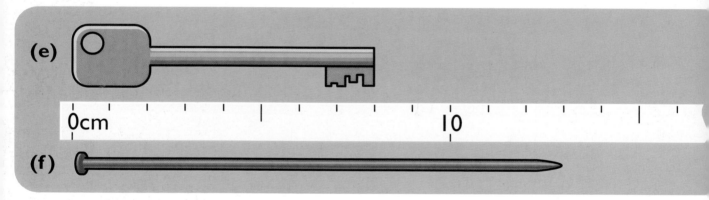

(e)

0cm 10

(f)

2 Measure each line. Write its length.

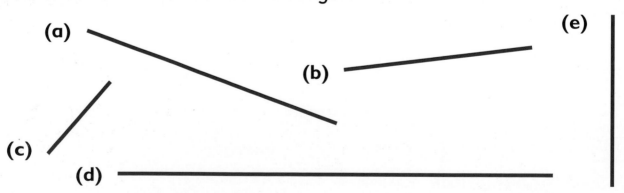

(a)

(b)

(c)

(d)

(e)

3 Draw lines of these lengths.

(a) 10 cm   (b) $3\frac{1}{2}$ cm   (c) 6 cm   (d) $12\frac{1}{2}$ cm

Use a tape measure and work with a friend.

3 |34 |35 |36 |37 |38 |39 |40 |41 |42 |43 |44 |45 |46 |47 |48 |49

1 Measure the distance around

(a) your head   **(b)** your neck   **(c)** your chest

  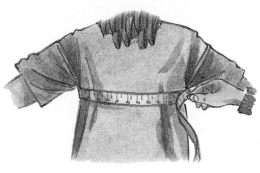

(d) your waist   **(e)** your wrist   **(f)** your ankle

(g) a bin   **(h)** a plastic bottle   **(i)** a hoop.

Use small counters.

1   How many counters are needed to cover each footprint?

(a) duck

(b) baby

(c) dog

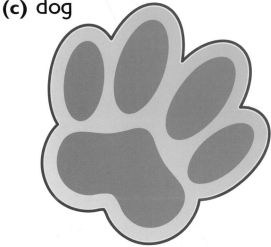

(d) cat

2   Which footprint covers
    (a) the greatest area
    (b) the smallest area?

3   How many counters are
    needed to cover **your** handprint?

1 Find the area of each shape in squares.

(a)

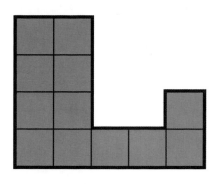

(b)

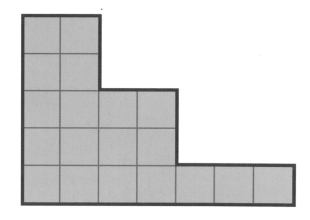

(c)

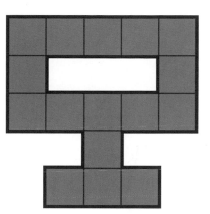

(d)

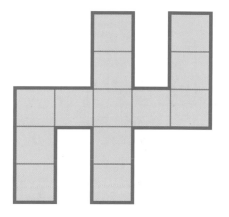

2 Which shape has
(a) the greatest area (b) the smallest area?

Use squared paper.

3 Draw and colour a shape
with an area of
(a) 10 squares
(b) 20 squares
(c) 30 squares.

4 Draw two **different** shapes each with an area of 24 squares.

Use water or sand, a  and a

I litre

$\frac{1}{2}$ litre

1 You need six containers like these.

Find which containers hold
(a) less than $\frac{1}{2}$ litre

(b) about $\frac{1}{2}$ litre

(c) more than $\frac{1}{2}$ litre.

I litre

$\frac{1}{2}$ litre

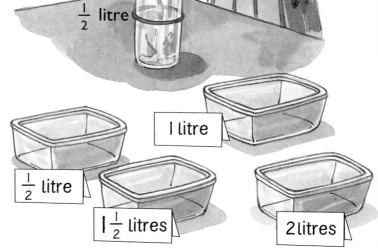

2 You need four tubs.

Measure into each
tub the amount on
its label.

I litre

$\frac{1}{2}$ litre

$1\frac{1}{2}$ litres

2 litres

3 You need three containers like these.

Estimate then measure how much each can hold.

1 How many litres of water are used altogether by
(a) Jake and Alex   (b) Alex and Kate   (c) all 3 children?

2 How many more litres of water are used by
(a) Kate than Alex   (b) Alex than Jake   (c) Kate than Jake?

3 How can Elsie measure 3 litres of water into the basin?
Find three different ways.

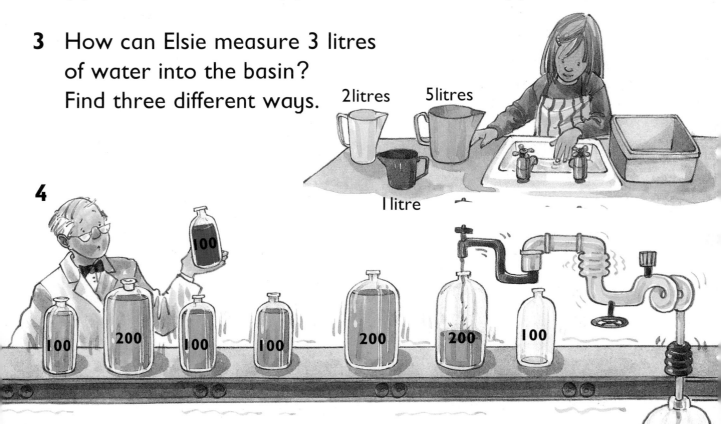

The bubble bath machine holds 1 litre.
How many of these bottles can be filled?
(a) 100 millilitre bottles   (b) 200 millilitre bottles

5 Find the different ways in which 100 **and** 200 millilitre bottles can be filled.

JULY

Sun	Mon	Tue	Wed	Thu	Fri	Sat
			1	2	3	4
5	6	7	8	9	10	11
12	13	14	15	16	17	18
19	20	21	22	23	24	25
26	27	28	29	30	31	

1 How many days of the month shown are
(a) Mondays   (b) Thursdays?

2 On which day of the week is
(a) 7th July   (b) twentieth July   (c) 31st July?

3 What day is it
(a) the day after 23rd July   (b) three days before 6th July
(c) one week after 4th July   (d) two weeks before 28th July?

4 What is the **date** on the
(a) third Wednesday of the month   (b) last Friday of the month?

5 What day of the week will the 1st of August be?

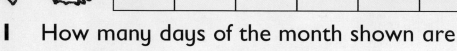

You need a calendar for **this year**.

6 Write the names of the months with (a) 31 days (b) 30 days.

7 On which day of the week is
(a) Christmas Day   (b) April Fool's Day   (c) New Year's Day?

1 Copy and complete each time.

(a)

quarter past __

(b)

quarter to __

(c)

half past __

(d)

__ o'clock

(e)

quarter to __

(f)

quarter past __

2 Write these times using

| o'clock | **or** | half past | **or** | quarter past | **or** | quarter to |

(a)

(b)

(c)

(d)

(e)

(f)

(g)

(h)

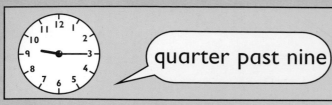 quarter past nine can be written as **9.15**

1 Write these times.

(a) 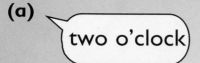 two o'clock

(b)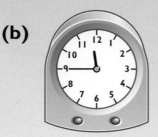

(c) quarter past six

(d)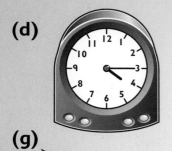

(e) half past twelve

(f)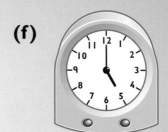

(g) quarter to eight

(h)

(i) quarter past two

2 Write

(a) the **earliest** time

  5:15   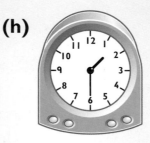 6:00

(b) the **latest** time.

  8:30     9:45

3 Write these times in order starting with the earliest.

8.00   7.45   6.30   7.15

Our Day Out by Class 3

On the bus
8.15 am

Eating our snack
12.30 pm

At the pond
2.15 pm

At the farm
9.00 am

In the park
10.45 am

Back to school
3.45 pm

1 Where was Class 3 **(a)** before 12 noon **(b)** after 12 noon?

2 Write these times. Use am or pm.

(a)

Quarter past ten

(b)

Eight o'clock

(c)

Half past three

(d)

Quarter to eleven in the morning.

(e)

Four o'clock in the afternoon.

3 Draw two things **you** do
(a) before 10.30 am
(b) after 4.45 pm.

The time is **5.40**.

1 Write each of these times.

(a)

(b)

(c)

(d)

(e)

(f)

(g) 20 minutes past 2

(h) 25 minutes to 11

(i) 10 minutes to 6

(j) 5 minutes to 9

(k) Quarter to 4

(l) 10 minutes past 7

2 Write in order, starting with the earliest.

6:40

Twenty-five minutes to eight.

Half past eight.

1 Write each time from Ruth's day in a **different way**.

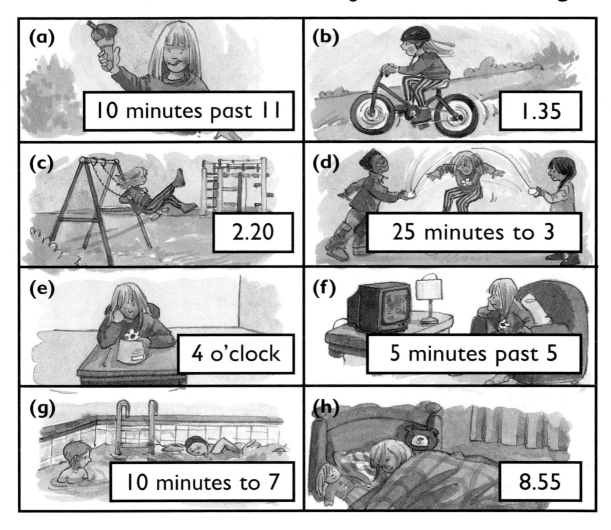

(a) 10 minutes past 11

(b) 1.35

(c) 2.20

(d) 25 minutes to 3

(e) 4 o'clock

(f) 5 minutes past 5

(g) 10 minutes to 7

(h) 8.55

2 Which colour of watch belongs to each child?

Sally: 25 minutes past 4.

Alma: 20 minutes to 5.

Tony: 20 minutes past 5.

Jane's bicycle trip log		
log entry	time	place
A	10.25 am	leave home
B	10.45 am	cross bridge
C	10.50 am	pass school
D	11.15 am	enter park
E	11.45 am	leave park
F	12.25 pm	return home

1 How many minutes are there between each entry in Jane's log?

2 How long after leaving home did she pass the school?

3 How long after crossing the bridge did she enter the park?

4 How long did Jane's bicycle trip take altogether?

5 Where was Jane at these times of the morning?

(a)

(b)

1 Matt leaves home at 8.25 am.
The journey to school takes 25 minutes.
At what time does he arrive?

2 A maths lesson starts at 9.20 am.
It finishes at 10.00 am.
How long does it last?

3 Morning break lasts for 20 minutes.
It ends at 10.50 am.
At what time does it start?

4 Complete the missing entries from Matt's afternoon timetable.

Activity	Starts at	Lasts for	Ends at
Lunch	12.45 pm	45 minutes	**(a)**
Reading	1.40 pm	**(b)**	2.10 pm
Art	**(c)**	40 minutes	3.20 pm

5 School ends at 3.30 pm.
Matt's swimming class starts 2 hours later.
The class lasts for 35 minutes.
At what time does it finish?

1 Find shapes like these.

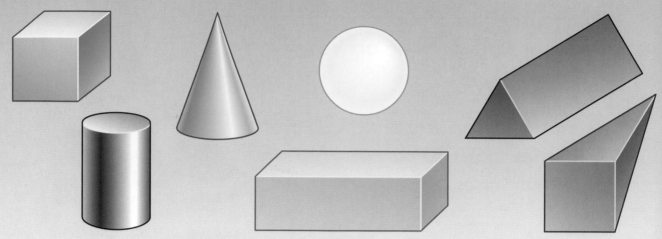

(a) Name each shape.

(b) Which shapes are **prisms**?

2 Name each of these shapes.

(a)

> I have one curved face and one flat face.

(b)

> I have twelve equal edges.

(c)

> I have two edges and no vertices.

(d)

> I have some triangular faces and six vertices.

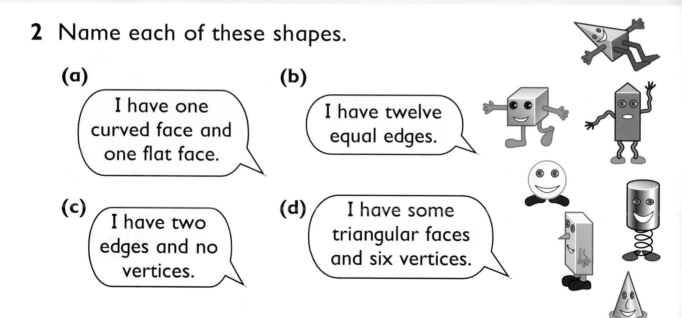

3 Write clues for each of these shapes.

(a)

(b)

1 Build shapes like these.

(a)

(b)

(c) 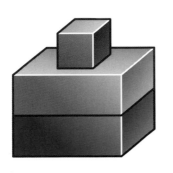   **(d)**    **(e)**

2 Which of these shapes are **not** prisms?

3 Use shapes like these.

(a) Build a prism.

(b) Sketch your prism.

(c) Build and sketch a different prism.

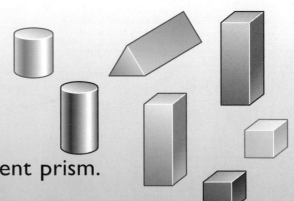

1 Use cubes to make these shapes.

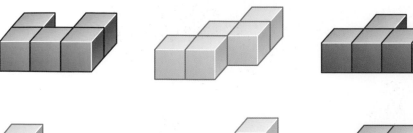

2 Make as many different shapes as you can using **four** cubes.

3 Tell a friend how to build these shapes.

Start with a large red cuboid...

1 Use two **triangles** to make each of these shapes.

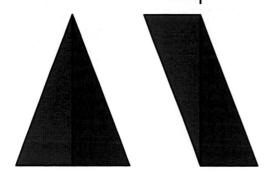

triangle　　**quadrilateral**　　　　　**hexagon**

2 Make then draw
(a) a different triangle　　(b) a different quadrilateral
(c) a different hexagon　　(d) a pentagon.

3 Use two **rectangles** to make each of these shapes.

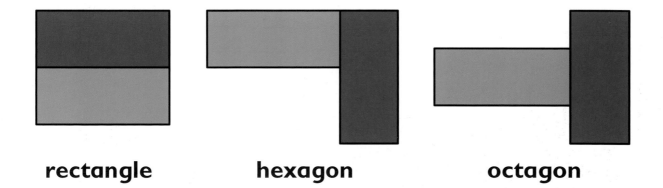

rectangle　　　　**hexagon**　　　　　**octagon**

4 Make then draw
(a) a different rectangle　　(b) a different octagon.

5 Use two **squares** to make then draw
(a) a rectangle　　(b) an octagon.

1 Draw what is at   **(a) B3**   **(b) D2**   **(c) A1**.

2 Write the positions of

(a)   (b)   (c) 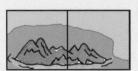   (d)   (e)

3 In which squares are there **trees**?

4 Write the squares the ▬▬ passes through. Start at **B3**.

island

North

West

reef

East

volcano

whale

South

raft

You are on the reef.

1 What do you see when you look **(a)** North **(b)** East?

2 In which direction is the **(a)** raft **(b)** volcano?

3 Face North.
What do you see when you turn through
(a) a right angle clockwise **(b)** a right angle anticlockwise
(c) a half turn **(d)** a whole turn?

4 Face West.
In which direction are you facing when you turn through
(a) 1 right angle anticlockwise **(b)** 3 right angles clockwise
(c) 2 right angles anticlockwise **(d)** 1 half turn?

5 Draw your own island with hills in the West, a tower in
the South, a wood in the North and a lake in the East.

1 How many lines of symmetry does each shape have?

(a)

(b)

(c)

(d)

(e)

(f)

2 How many lines of symmetry does each letter have?

Which shape completes the symmetrical letter?

3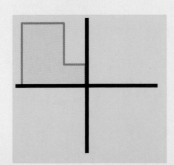

(a)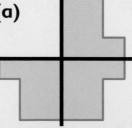

(b)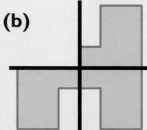

(c)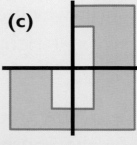

4

(a)

(b)

(c)

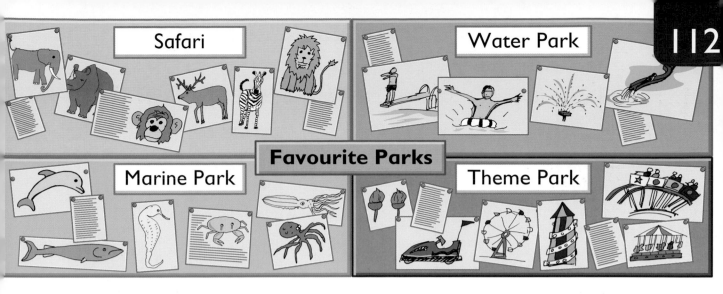

Safari

Water Park

Favourite Parks

Marine Park

Theme Park

1 Class 3 visited four parks.

(a) Which park was
  • most popular
  • least popular?

(b) Which parks had
  • more than 7 votes
  • less than 7 votes?

(c) How many children voted for parks with animals?

Favourite Parks

Park	Votes
Safari	5
Water	8
Theme	10
Marine	7

2 (a) Find out which of the 4 parks children in your class would most like to visit.

(b) List your results in a table.

(c) Which park is
  • most popular
  • least popular?

(d) How many children voted for **either** the Water Park **or** the Theme Park?

Park	Votes
Safari	

Ghost Boats

Number of children (y-axis): 0–10

Spooky · Scary · Slimy · Creepy

1 How many children rode
   (a) on Spooky   **(b)** on Scary
   (c) on Slimy   **(d)** altogether?

2 How many fewer children rode on
   (a) Scary than Spooky
   (b) Creepy than Slimy
   (c) Spooky than Slimy?

3 On which boat was the number of children
   (a) greatest   **(b)** smallest
   (c) an even number
   (d) two more than on Spooky
   (e) double the number on Scary
   (f) the same as the number in
         Scary and Creepy together?

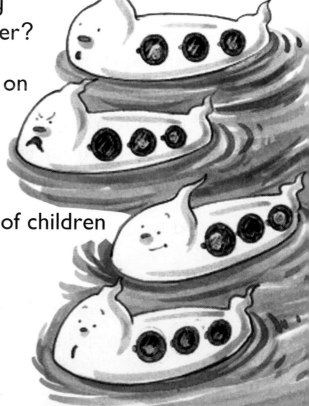

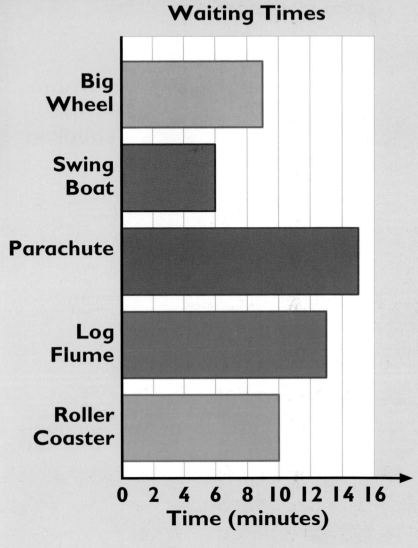

Waiting Times

1 Which ride has the shortest waiting time?

2 Which ride has a waiting time of
(a) 10 minutes
(b) 13 minutes
(c) 9 minutes
(d) 15 minutes?

3 How much longer is the wait for the Parachute than for the
(a) Log Flume (b) Swing Boat (c) Big Wheel?

4 Why do you think each ride has a different waiting time?

1 Which neck style is
   (a) most common
   (b) least common?

Neck style

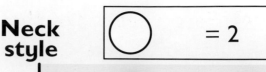 = 2

2 How many children
   have these styles?

Number of children

(a)  (b) 🖤

(c) 👕 (d) 👕

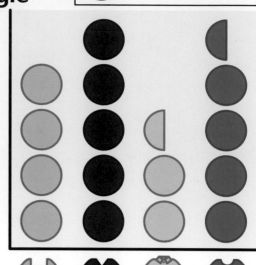

3 How many children
   are there altogether?

4 Which style is twice as common as 👕 ?

⭕ = 2 children

Patterns

  plain 🔺

  striped 🔺

  checked 🔺

  hooped 🔺

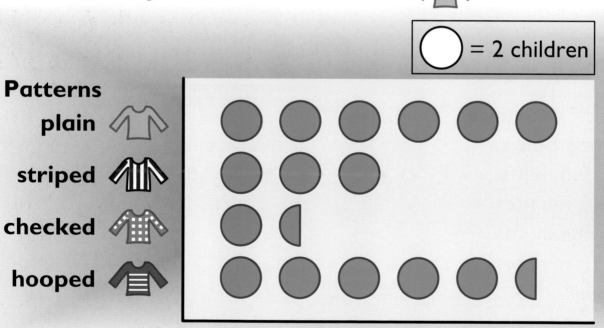

Number of tops

5 How many tops are
   (a) plain   (b) striped   (c) checked   (d) hooped?

6 Which pattern is on half as many tops as
   (a) the plain pattern   (b) the striped pattern?

1 (a) Sort a set of flat shapes
into two sets:

(b) Draw the shapes in a
diagram like this:

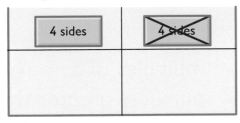

(c) List the shapes with 4 sides.

2 (a) Try to sort the shapes into four sets:

(b) Draw the shapes in a diagram like this:

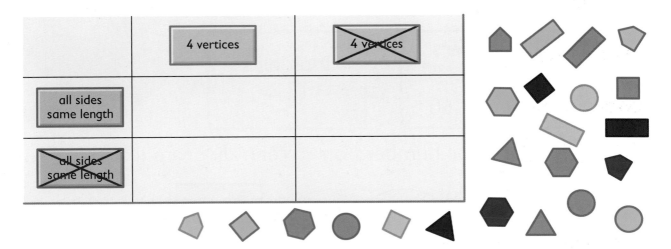

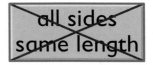

(c) Name a shape
• with 4 vertices **and** all sides the same length
• which does not have 4 vertices **and**
does not have all sides the same length.

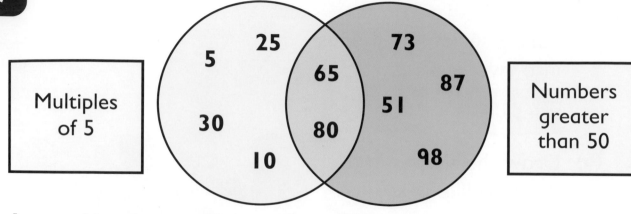

1 (a) List three other numbers for

- the yellow part ⟶ multiples of 5
- the blue part ⟶ numbers greater than 50
- the green part ⟶ multiples of 5 **and** numbers greater than 50.

(b) In which part should 50 go? Explain.

2 (a) List 8, 23, 32, 71 and 12 other numbers less than 80.

(b) Sort your numbers into two sets:

Numbers between 20 and 60

Multiples of 4

(c) Write your numbers on a Venn diagram like this:

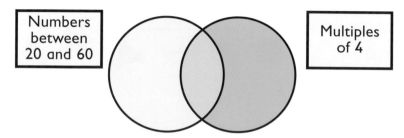

(d) Which numbers did **not** fit inside the circles? Why not?